# Managing Conflict

## GILL TAYLOR

DIRECTORY OF SOCIAL CHANGE

Published by:
The Directory of Social Change
24 Stephenson Way
London NW1 2DP
Tel: 0171 209 5151, Fax: 0171 209 5049
E-mail: info@dsc.org.uk
from whom further copies and a full publications list are available

The Directory of Social Change is a Registered Charity no. 800517

First published 1999
Copyright © The Directory of Social Change 1999

ISBN 1 900360 28 4

British Library Cataloguing in Publication Data
A catalogue record for this book is available from the British Library

Cover design by Kenny Mansley
Designed and typeset by Sarah Nicholson
Printed and bound by Page Bros., Norwich

Directory of Social Change London Office:
Courses and Conferences tel: 0171 209 4949
Charityfair tel: 0171 209 1015
Research tel: 0171 209 4422
Finance and Administration tel: 0171 209 0902

Directory of Social Change Northern Office:
3rd Floor, Federation House, Hope Street, Liverpool L1 9BW
Research tel: 0151 708 0136
Courses and Conferences tel: 0151 708 0117

# CONTENTS

# ACKNOWLEDGEMENTS

I would like to thank my readers Paul Ticher, Sarah Hargreaves, Helen Carmichael.

Extracts from *Playing with Fire* by Nic Fine and Fiona Macbeth, reproduced with permission from LEAP Confronting Conflict.

Extracts from *Just about Managing*, reproduced with the permission of Sandy Adirondack.

Extracts from *Playing with Fire* and *From Strength to Strength*, reproduced with the permission of Youth Work Press and National Youth Agency, Leicester.

All Scenarios are created from imagination and experience arising from several situations. Any resemblance to organisations, teams, or individuals is entirely accidental and certainly not intentional.

## Introduction

This book is written for:

- managers who are managing conflicts within their teams;
- employees who have to handle conflict at work with colleagues or with clients, residents or users;
- those who feel less confident at handling team conflicts than they would like;
- those who are faced with a situation they find does not respond to their usual strategies.

It aims to provide:

insight into how conflict arises

ideas about how to understand each particular conflict situation

an opportunity for readers to analyse their normal reaction to conflict

a range of techniques both for individual employees and for managers that can be effective in resolving conflict.

There are three main aspects to a successful resolution of any conflict:

each individual's *personal response* to the conflict and their skills in handling it

any *external environmental or organisational factors* that might be contributing

a *manager's responsibility for providing a framework* for handling team conflicts.

All of these issues will be covered in detail in Part 1.

The skills that help us to cope successfully with conflict do not come naturally to us all. However, everyone can learn to recognise what's going on in a conflict situation. By analysing each incident more carefully we can learn how to get a more positive outcome. It is also possible to learn to recognise the basic motivations and differences that create and fuel conflict. Understanding the rules of negotiation and mediation and developing a toolkit of techniques and strategies are the keys to getting more positive outcomes more often.

It would not be realistic to expect to go from a situation where most experiences of conflict are negative straight to one where most experience is neutral or positive. It requires thinking more clearly about what is going on in each situation, being aware of feelings or nuances of expression and then acting appropriately in response to that new awareness. Learning these skills takes time.

If you are reading this book, it may be because you feel you are not a natural at conflict resolution. The good news is that there are skills and techniques you can learn. Once acquired, these will prove invaluable in your everyday life both at work and outside the workplace.

*Managing Conflict* is organised in two parts.

Part 1 covers the issues outlined above in five chapters.

1   What is conflict?
2   Conflict at work
3   Team and organisational factors
4   Personal responses to conflict
5   Techniques for handling conflict

Part 2 contains twelve scenarios that describe common workplace conflict situations. They invite the reader to explore the factors contributing to each situation and to consider how they can best be handled or resolved using conflict resolution skills, either by managers or by employees themselves.

The scenarios are based on the actions of managers and staff in three fictional voluntary sector organisations. They cover five themes of conflict:

Power imbalances within an organisation
Problematic relations with clients
Team dynamics
Differences between individuals
Managing change

This book and the scenarios in it arise out of my experience as a personnel manager and consultant working with teams and managers in the voluntary sector. There is no one theoretical background that underpins it – rather it is informed by my observations of teams and human nature. My goal has been to provide ideas and suggestions for practical problem solving.

The *Further Reading* section at the end has ideas for where to read about a psychological or group work approach to conflict.

# WHAT IS CONFLICT?

## Introduction

Conflict is all around us: in our homes, at work, in the street; it is reported in the media and forms the substance of drama; it occurs between individuals, groups, or countries. Conflict is a normal, or certainly very pervasive, condition in our society.

Conflict has negative connotations for most people most of the time. It provokes more negative word associations and negative feelings than positive ones. However, conflict outcomes do not have to be negative for either or both parties involved. They can be positive: stimulating, thoughtful, creative and empowering. A positive outcome (in the context of the workplace) is one where:

- both parties have been able to air their differences or disagreements fully;
- each party has been heard by the other;
- both have their views recognised if not agreed with;
- and a resolution is found that both can work with, and which does not demean or diminish one of the parties.

The goal in dealing with conflict at work for those who feel less skilled at present is to get more positive outcomes more often. That is the central theme of this book, and one that will be explored fully in the remaining chapters of Part 1.

## Definitions

So how can we define conflict? Here are three different definitions that highlight different facets of the word:

> Conflict occurs when two or more parties believe that what each wants is incompatible with what the other wants.
>
> Conflict arises when differences cannot be satisfactorily dealt with.
>
> Chinese characters for conflict are Opportunity – Danger

- The first definition emphasises that different perspectives of the participants may influence the outcome of conflict.
- The second stresses that it is about dealing with differences.
- The third covers the idea of positive as well as negative potentials of conflict.

## Different perspectives

There are going to be different perspectives on the causes of the conflict from each participant. There are also going to be different attitudes to the simple fact of 'being in a conflict'. Everyone has to deal with conflict, whether as an individual or in a group, as a participant, negotiator or mediator. Some people don't seem to regard the tension negatively, or seem to thrive on conflict; others find it stressful and try to resist or avoid it; others absorb all the stresses into themselves, taking on too much responsibility for solving the conflict. This may make it seem twice as bad as it is.

## Dealing with difference

Everyone is different: human dynamics consist of varying mixes of dependency, creativity, aggression and support. That's what makes us interesting, but also what leads to differing views. Differences are based on our individual sense of identity, which is deep seated and has grown up from each interaction with the world.

In any group or team relationship there will also be differences. People think differently, have different values, interpret information in different ways. Differences are the basis on which individuals, relationships and organisations grow and change. Sameness may seem attractive, but in the end it can lead to stagnation and complacency.

In a society that supports its members, if they are to live and work happily and securely, people need to be able to resolve their differences without unnecessary violence or aggression. If staff are to work well together in teams, organisations need to support them in dealing with difference and in developing skills to resolve conflicts without dis-empowering team members.

## Conflict always stems from differences

Differences exist and won't go away. Conflict arises when differences are not recognised or are badly handled. For example:

1    The senior manager wants the line managers to take responsibility for health and safety risk assessments in their detached offices. The line managers perceive this as inappropriate delegation of a senior responsibility and no training has been offered to them to carry out the

assessments. The senior manager imposes the change on them and the line managers either do not carry it out or do so reluctantly. The consequences are potential infringement of health and safety legislation; increased risk to staff and users; distrust between senior and line managers.

In this case the main difference is how the participants perceive the manager's role at senior and line manager level (of course other factors also contribute to the conflict).

2    One worker in the office only ever washes up a cup when they need one and never washes up anyone else's cups. Another worker is not happy to leave the office unless the washing up is all done and the towels are neat and tidy. Tension builds up until the 'neat and tidy' person accuses the other worker of being lazy and selfish.

The differences here are both attitudes to neatness, tidiness and office cleanliness; and expectations about how much communal effort is required from individual staff to ensure the smooth running of the office. A small instance of lack of respect or what is perceived as lack of respect, can blow a conflict up very quickly out of proportion to the originating remark or incident.

## Effective teams can deal with difference

Effective organisations or teams can cope with differences. There is a sense of unity, of commitment to common objectives or ideals, but there is also a sense of diversity. Differences are welcomed and there are clear opportunities to express and discuss differing views.

This does not mean that everyone can always get what they want. People must recognise that working together as a group means that sometimes they have to do things they do not want, or go along with decisions they do not fully agree with.

The potential for conflict is ever present. But, if we find that conflict is leading too often to outcomes that are either negative for us or negative for others we deal with, then we need a strategy to improve our performance.

## Positive and negative potential

### Conflict need not have negative outcomes

Conflict will inevitably have harmful outcomes or be destructive where it is resolved by oppression or by one side not taking full account of the other's position and opinions. This will create resentments, whether they are expressed or unexpressed. It can lead to a cycle of encounters which heap resentment on resentment. Service to users may also be adversely affected. Examples of negative outcomes are:

- some people may feel defeated and demeaned;
- the distance between people may be increased;
- a climate of distrust and suspicion may develop;
- turbulence may cause valued people to leave;
- dealing with difference may reinforce stereotypes or oppressive practices;
- people or departments that ought to co-operate may become concerned with only their narrow interests;
- active or passive resistance may develop where teamwork is needed.

(List from 'Handling Conflict' in *From Strength to Strength*, see *Further Reading*.)

## Differences can lead to conflict

Differences become conflict with negative potential in the following situations.

- Participants are reluctant to accept the validity of differing values, priorities or views of what is right or important.
- Individuals or the group as a whole have different or unclear standards for action, behaviour or performance and common standards cannot be agreed.
- Something (money, attention, workload, responsibility) is, or is perceived to be, unfairly distributed.
- Participants act on an individual or collective need to win, be right, get their own way or dominate.
- Participants succumb to fear, distrust and the need to define anyone different or unknown as 'other', 'outsider' or 'the enemy'.
- Participants do not want to change.
- There are unclear or non-existent procedures for discussing and resolving differences before they escalate into conflict.

(List from 'Managing Conflict' in *Just about Managing*, see *Further Reading*.)

# Turning negative outcomes into positive ones

Some people find conflict difficult, upsetting or scary, but the outcome need not be negative. It can release creativity and lead to positive outcomes. For this to happen, the participants must stop and work through the opposing ideas and issues in a careful measured way. They must respect each other's right to be different without allowing that difference to become harmful.

For the person trying to help resolve a conflict, it is important to focus on the potentials and positive outcomes that can be achieved. Some examples are:

- better ideas are produced;
- participants are forced to search for new approaches;

- long-standing problems surface and are dealt with;
- participants are forced to clarify points of view;
- the tension of conflict stimulates interest and activity;
- participants can go away feeling good about, and respected for, their opinions;
- participants have a chance to test their capabilities.

(List from 'Handling Conflict' in *From Strength to Strength*, see *Further Reading*.)

The goal of understanding and managing conflict is to increase the likelihood that such benefits will be secured. The first task is to consider some definitions of conflict and then to examine more closely examine how conflicts arise. Next we can begin to equip ourselves with the tools to analyse better and in more detail 'What's going on?'. This is covered in Chapters 3 and 4.

> **In summary: when dealing with conflict there are four important points to remember**
> Conflict is not inevitable but differences are.
> Conflict arises when differences cannot be accommodated.
> Conflict outcomes do not have to be negative and destructive.
> Conflict outcomes can be creative and positive.

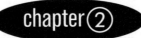

# CONFLICT AT WORK

## Introduction

There are four main influences on the causes of conflict at work:

- The process and relationships in which managers and employees find themselves (*Group and Organisational*).
- Management skills and management culture in the workplace (*Managerial*).
- Each individual's style in relation to conflict and whether or not we find it easy to work with each other – our pattern (*Individual*).
- The background/style and values individuals inherit (*Cultural*).

While Chapter 4 looks at the individual and cultural processes at work, Chapter 3 deals with the managerial, work environment and organisational factors influencing conflict. These can sometimes be so powerful as to make the situation feel out of control.

The workplace is a rich source of opportunities for conflict. There are many differences that can and should be expressed in a healthy organisation. These include:

- individual employees' relationships with each other;
- relationships up and down the hierarchy;
- the team's internal differences;
- the relationship between the team and other teams or individuals inside the organisation;
- the team and its relationships with clients, customers, residents, users;
- the team's relationship with their manager.

Paradoxically it is usual to spend more waking hours in contact with colleagues than with family and friends. Conflict that is not easy to resolve or which often resurfaces, can be a great contributor to stress at work and makes the organisation ineffective. It is therefore vital that managers take conflict seriously and learn how to deal with it.

Other factors such as the work environment can affect people's inclination to resolve conflicts. The structure of the organisation, the relationship between the senior staff and Trustees, and the effectiveness of channels of communication all have an impact both on how conflict arises and how effectively it is resolved. Employees' relationships with their managers and colleagues in the team, however, probably have the most enduring influence.

Another challenge for any manager is to be more aware of the interpersonal processes that can affect the build up to a conflict. To do this we need both to understand the likely patterns and history relating to conflict, and to be more aware and analytical about what is going on before we leap into sorting it out.

In any case, successful intervention in conflict requires the manager:

- to understand the processes which give rise to conflict;
- to recognise what kinds of behaviour drive or fuel it;
- to look at team behaviour in particular;
- to consider organisational factors;
- to know how to choose and apply appropriate responses to difficult situations.

The first four points are covered in the following pages and the last point is covered in Chapter 5.

Chapter 5 details a toolkit of response strategies. As we become more skilled in dealing with different conflict situations it is easier to know instinctively how to apply the different responses, and which has the best chance of getting a positive response for yourself and the other participants. (Bear in mind that there may be an interim position which is to back off, stand back, allow a cooling off period, rather than forcing people to resolve matters instantly – especially if there are heated arguments.)

# Understanding the processes

Learning about the processes that occur in conflict can aid managers and help participants understand more about what is going on.

- Most conflicts at work involve people already known to each other. Only conflicts with clients or users of the organisation are going to involve strangers. This creates a particular type of influence on behaviour, where 'baggage' carried between the two individuals in conflict may carry on from one episode to the next. This explains why, in dealing with some conflicts, it feels as though the participants need to go back to the year dot to find any satisfactory resolution. (See Model 1 below.)
- The internal dialogue and dynamic are different for each individual. One person's conflict with difficult emotional consequences is another person's brush off. This is why there can be no single right way to resolve a conflict. The individuals in each case need to be taken into consideration.

- There can be different perceptions about what is going on, as participants see the same incident from different angles or power positions. Radically different explanations as to what is going on and radically different solutions may seem 'right' to each person concerned. In this case the participants need to be encouraged to think about it from the other's point of view.
- Conflicts can be driven by other forces and escalate quickly beyond the original spark of difference. In this case people can be seen as fuel and the potential escalation as a conflagration. (See Model 2 below.)
- There may also be organisational or environmental factors at work that need addressing before the conflict can be resolved.

Each conflict involves a set of building blocks and perspectives that influence how traumatic it is, how easy to understand and resolve. Some conflicts can be very complex and have hidden layers of difference underneath more obvious ones. Some of these factors are obvious, some are hidden, some are easily agreed on, some depend on individual perceptions:

Individual difference
People and their individual patterns in relation to conflict
Team factors
Organisational factors
Management culture.

Conflict is also dynamic in nature. It very rarely involves just one incident or just two people. The following two models reflect the dynamic nature of conflict.

## Two models for describing the dynamics of inter-personal conflict

### Model 1 Conflict as episode

One way to describe conflict is as a series of episodes – like the continuing plot of a soap opera. Each encounter has a shape and an outcome, and involves the participants in communication that is usually felt as unsatisfactory by one or both participants. The next time the participants encounter each other they are not coming in fresh. They have a memory of the previous meeting and the unsatisfactory way it happened. This will then influence their behaviour and expectations of the other's behaviour. The less satisfactory each encounter is, the more the interactions can spiral out of control towards destructive or negative patterns. When this occurs among a team which has to work closely together it can be very debilitating. Sometimes it can escalate, with more and more people 'taking sides'.

The individuals typically lack the skills to resolve it, or to see in a balanced way what is going on for themselves or for the other party to the conflict. Other people may be involved tangentially, watching what is going on or using the key participants to represent dissatisfactions of their own that they feel disinclined to put on the table themselves.

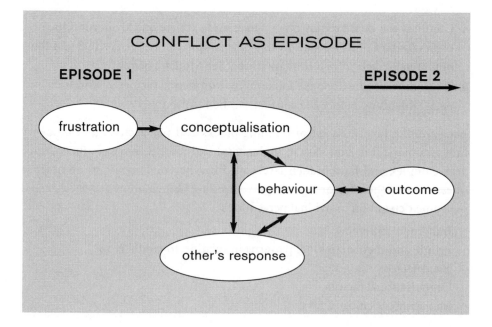

**Frustration** occurs when a person has a clear feeling that someone or some group is getting in the way.

**Conceptualisation** involves answering the questions 'What's going on here?' and 'What's the problem?' and forms the basis of one's reaction to frustration. The way parties define the problem has a great deal of influence over the chances of a constructive outcome.

**Behaviour** is the result of the answers to the conceptualisation questions. People form a strategy and set in motion a pattern of interaction. The longer the pattern continues, the more the actions of the participants themselves may create new frustrations.

**Outcome** is the state of affairs that exists at the end of an episode, including decisions or actions taken and the feelings of the parties involved.
A useful way of evaluating the outcome is to consider the quality of the action or decision that results, the condition of the conflicting parties at the end of the conflict and the quality of the relationship between the conflicting parties.

'Understanding the conflict process' comes from *From Strength to Strength*. See *Further Reading*.

## Example

The scenario that follows illustrates the model in action. It is set in a small organisation dealing with providing services to local elderly people and has four staff: a manager, a volunteer co-ordinator, an information officer and an administrator. The information officer is new in post.

### ▶ Frustration

An elderly client has complained about the inappropriate behaviour of one of the volunteers. The complaint has been made to the information officer (Kelly). The manager is away on holiday for two weeks. Kelly has a very strong idea about how to work with volunteers and has been on training courses in her previous post. She believes that while it is important to build a relationship with volunteers this does not mean that you have to accept poor performance. She feels that the complaint should be dealt with through formal procedures. The current volunteer co-ordinator (June) has been in post for ten years and knows the volunteers really well personally. She feels it is important to take an individual approach and does not want to upset them all by making them feel that they are in the wrong.

### ▶ Conceptualisation

Kelly perceives that June is too 'cosy' with the volunteers and she thinks she has lost her 'edge' or authority over them. She worries that poor performance could damage the contract they have with social services and harm their professional image in the local area. Kelly feels that June doesn't understand this. June perceives Kelly to be a young, jumped up, know-it-all, who has no right to rock boats. June sees Kelly's approach as overly bureaucratic. Incidents normally get sorted by her having a quiet word in the volunteer's ear. She sees the threat to the organisation as being from bad feeling among the volunteers. Bad mouthing in the community could result in the loss of her workforce.

### ▶ Behaviour

Kelly decides to bring up the issue face to face with June one lunchtime. Kelly feels that her perception of the problem is confirmed and tells June that her approach to volunteers is out-dated and potentially dangerous. June begins to raise her voice and uses increasingly angry language with Kelly. 'Jumped up interfering new girl' is how she rounds off the discussion, and then walks out. June is confirmed in her view of Kelly and thinks she has no idea of the real difficulties of being in her shoes as volunteer co-ordinator. After all, the whole organisation would crumble without 'her' volunteers.

▶ **Outcome**

Kelly is furious at June's response. She goes to the manager, now back from holiday, to talk about the issue and the lack of respect June showed her in the lunchtime discussion. Kelly thinks that her working relationship with June is now going to be 'difficult' and has no faith in June co-operating with her. The manager also has an account of the incident from June, but has no chance to resolve it before June and Kelly next meet in the office.

**EPISODE 2**

▶ **Conceptualisation**

This incident now influences how Kelly and June either change their behaviour towards each other or confirm their perceptions of what's going on. The history of the relationship cannot be forgotten in approaching the next interaction. Each separate episode could result in escalating tension, lack of trust and lack of respect, despite intervention from the manager.

# Model 2: Conflict as fire

This model comes from work that has been developed into a training model for use especially with young people by LEAP Confronting Conflict. They have published the training guide *Playing with Fire* with the National Youth Agency Press (see *Further Reading*). It encourages participants to see the work of confronting conflict as something daring, exciting and challenging. In the development of the role, young people find it more powerful to use the image of firefighter than of peace maker. The analogy can facilitate a memorably quick analysis of the stages of conflict; and it can help us to see conflict like fire, as a good servant and a bad master.

It is a good analogy to use where the whole team or whole organisation is in conflict and it has escalated, involving more and more people. In the scenario described below managers' incompetence adds to the conflict.

# CONFLICT AS FIRE

## CONFLICT

### ▶ People

Whenever people are in contact with each other, there is potential for conflict. This potential will vary according to the different degrees of combustibility of the individuals.

### ▶ Incident

There are always tensions and disagreements between people. Some of them can cause a spark which ignites conflict.

### ▶ Brooding

Tensions and grievances are smouldering away but are unexpressed. The conflict feeds off rumour and gossip.

### ▶ Aggravation

Those who are interested in agitating the situation provoke it further. Feelings of anger and hurt may be expressed in prejudice and hate.

### ▶ Escalation

The situation is intensified by the outside pressures of the social environment. Prejudice and disaffection add to the conflict.

### ▶ Consequences

There is a blazing conflict in which some people are damaged. No one involved is untouched by it.

## FIRE

### ▶ The fuel

The raw material of the fire. Some of it is highly combustible. Some of it is damp and flame resistant.

### ▶ The spark

Friction causes sparks to fly. Some land on dry wood and it catches alight.

### ▶ Smouldering

The fuel catches alight and begins to smoke. There is an indication of fire.

### ▶ Fanning the flames

The wind blows and the smouldering fuel flickers with life. The flames lick and leap.

### ▶ Stroking the fire

The fire consumes the fuel. It demands more. Huge logs are piled onto the fire.

### ▶ The blaze

The fire rages. It is a huge blaze. It will not die down easily.

## CHANGE

### ▶ People

Whenever people are in contact with each other, there is potential for challenge and growth. Different values, opinions or aims contain raw issues and fuel for fire.

### ▶ Flash of insight

There are always raw issues in a community or relationship. Sometimes a flash of new insight can bring an issue alive for an individual.

### ▶ Tentative response

The individual looks for shared concern from others, making an initial response to the issue.

### ▶ Encouraged action

Those showing concern for the issue grow in number, encouraging and supporting each other.

### ▶ Increased response

Response to the issue increases. The possibilities of achievement inspire action from many.

### ▶ Effective action

Aims are achieved. People celebrate the blazing fire. It is a beacon which lights warms and inspires.

(Fire Model from *Playing with Fire*, see *Further Reading*.)

### Example

An organisation of 60 staff providing advice and services to young homeless people has four main teams: Finance & Administration, Advice & Information, Housing & Hostels, and Campaigning.

#### ► Incident and spark

The advice team has just been told by their senior manager that they have to move to a newly refurbished part of the building which is an open-plan office. The team has not been told about this before, or been consulted on the move.

#### ► Brooding and Smouldering

The team is not happy. They go out together for lunch and decide that they do not like the idea of the move. They are angry that this has been sprung on them, and an open-plan office is simply not going to facilitate advice work, where they need to hold conversations in relative privacy. Members of the campaigning team join them and suggest this is a 'political' move because the Finance Director lobbied very hard for his team not to go into the open-plan office. The advice team concludes that their manager is clearly not doing his job properly. They decide to send a representative group to the manager to complain.

#### ► Aggravation, fanning the flames

The manager receives the delegation, who begin by aggressively suggesting that the manager has let them down, that he can't do his job properly and that the team has been stitched up with the least attractive and suitable office space because of his weak negotiation skills. He compares unfavourably with the Finance Director. This approach does not go down well with the manager. He says he does not like being spoken to like this, accuses them of being rude and paranoid, digs his heels in and says there is no option about the move: it will happen next week.

#### ► Escalation, stoking the fire

The senior managers meet to discuss the office move and decide that on objective grounds it is still best for the advice team to move. They can have partitions to block the noise levels if they are too high. The senior manager of the advice team mentions the grievances of his team and is told to manage them into agreement – not to let a little local difficulty get in the way of the Chief Executive's plans. 'Surely you have your team under control, James?' is one of the comments made. Meanwhile the advice team decides to consult their union representative about the implications of the move and whether they can be required to move. They decide to make a formal complaint via the union and threaten to go on strike if they are not consulted.

## ▶ Consequences, the blaze

The Chief Executive has to get involved in negotiations with the Union –
feeling, however, that this is a waste of time and a consequence of James'
poor management techniques. James, the advice team manager, feels let
down by his team and his boss and reflects on the iniquitous position of
middle management. He fears that his reputation is on the line, which leads
him to be either aggressive or conciliatory by turns. The team feels let
down, unheard and forced to resort to their ultimate threat of taking formal
union action. They now do not trust the line manager to consult them, see
him as an ineffective character in the cut and thrust of internal politics, and
begin to treat his management instructions with contempt.

chapter ③

# TEAM AND ORGANISATIONAL FACTORS

## Understanding behaviour

As a manager or team member, it can be particularly useful to begin to 'people watch' a little more dispassionately than usual and to begin to recognise patterns emerging not only in yourself, but in others around you. Neither of the team situations described in Chapter 2 need necessarily lead to conflict with negative outcomes. The mix usually needs more ingredients added before conflict arises. Some of the behaviours that drive or fuel conflict are:

■ not listening
■ not acting
■ taking dramatic action
■ being contemptuous of the others' positions or views
■ inappropriate use of language, power, position or knowledge
■ telling stories behind people's backs
■ oppression
■ harassment
■ making assumptions about others' motives or the nature or reasons for differences
■ not owning your own opinion
■ resentments or jealousy
■ fear of being shown up or criticised
■ being/feeling disempowered
■ blaming and not owning feelings
■ not taking appropriate responsibility
■ different ideas about confidentiality.

This is my base line list of behaviours – I'm sure you can add to it!

The best tactic is to learn to be more skilled at recognising and naming what is going on and then pointing it out to participants. Once behaviour is noticed, this is half way to dealing more positively with it. An individual may be able to analyse what is going on but have fears about acting: this is more long term and complex to deal with, and may involve strategies for gaining allies.

# Teams as groups

Most people in an organisation work in teams. A team is a group of people put together in a logical organisational unit, either by location or by work type and content. Some tasks may be shared out among group members and some may be allocated to individuals within the group, but the group as a whole relies on tasks being achieved to function effectively.

Most managers have to manage people in groups rather than as lone workers. Groups have been the subject of academic studies for decades, leading to a better understanding of group characteristics.

Managers can use this both to understand some of the things that happen in teams and to manage the inevitable conflicts better. Here are some key points:

- Individuals spend most of their lives in groups from the family onwards.
- Managers are dealing with people who have already been shaped by previous group experiences and as such are not a 'blank sheet of paper'.
- As a team member or manager you can't usually choose all your team or your management colleagues.
- Teams have both internal relationships and external relationships with other teams or the group hierarchy.

All these characteristics offer a wide opportunity for difference to lead to tension, disfunction and conflict with negative outcomes. However, teams may have more conflict but produce better results overall if they are heterogeneous rather than homogenous. Diversity tends towards productivity, unity towards stagnation.

# Group (team) characteristics that can exacerbate conflict

As a manager it is vital to be aware of the following eight major characteristics of groups – which are therefore likely to affect teams. When conflicts arise it will be important to keep them in mind as likely causes or contributing factors. It is unlikely that a manager will face all of these or even more than two in any one team at any one time, but knowing they are potential characteristics may give you an added edge in sorting out the conflict in the best possible way.

Some of the following characteristics are illustrated in the scenarios in Part 2.

## 1 Group norms, culture and etiquette

All group members develop a set of norms – expected ways of behaving within the group which are established either informally or formally. The norms express the values of the group's members and provide the group with the means to achieve its goals. Norms might be:

- whether the group members greet each other in the morning or not;
- length of tea break;
- amount of self exploitation and not taking time off in lieu;
- time keeping.

Individuals who wish to go against the group norm have several alternatives. If they have high status, they may get away with being different. They may even manage to change the norm. They may be tolerated if they benefit the group in other ways or they may face sanctions and be persuaded to conform. There are lots of group pressures on an individual, and in deciding whether to conform to the group norms, individuals can chose to:

- comply as a means of convenience but not conviction;
- fully accept the group norms;
- reject the norms or the group or both.

No member of the group is likely to be completely happy with all the norms of a group, and any form of disagreement has the potential for conflict. (See *Scenarios 1.1, 3.2.*)

## 2 Stages of group development

Groups have certain cyclical inevitabilities.

The following four well-known stages have been defined.

*Forming:* The group is still a set of individuals. This stage is characterised by talk about the purpose of the group, its definition and composition, its lifestyle and characteristics. At this stage each individual wants to establish their personal identity within the group and make some individual impression.

*Storming:* This is the conflict stage where the preliminary consensus on purposes, leadership roles and other boundaries of the group are challenged. At this point any personal agendas might be revealed and a certain amount of interpersonal hostility is generated. If successfully handled, this stage leads to a new and more realistic setting of objectives, procedures and norms.

*Norming:* The group needs to establish norms and practices: when and how it should work, how it should take decisions, what type of behaviour, what level of work, what degree of openness, trust and confidence is appropriate. At this stage there may be tentative experimentation by individuals to test the temperature of the group and to measure the appropriate level of commitment.

> *Performing:* Only when the three previous stages have been successfully completed will the group be at full maturity and be able to be fully and sensibly productive. Some kind of performance will be achieved at all stages of development, but it is likely to be impeded by the other processes of growth and by individual agendas. In many periodic committees, the leadership issue or the objective and purpose of the group are recurring topics that crop up in every meeting, seriously hindering the true work of the group.

(From *Understanding Organisations*, see *Further Reading*.)

Some managers are better than others at being aware of group processes. Some shy away from drawing attention to them even if they are aware of them, for fear of wasting time or being accused of encouraging the team to 'navel gaze'. It is not self indulgent to notice group interaction and cycles and make any tensions and issues explicit. Many conflicts arise because of dysfunctional group interactions, and hence get even more in the way of the team's service delivery.

## 3 Group think

L. Janis defined 'Group Think' as the 'psychological drive for consensus at any cost that suppresses dissent and appraisal of alternatives in cohesive decision making groups.' (From *Victims of Group Think*, see *Further Reading*.)

Janis studied several high-profile American foreign policy disasters including the Bay of Pigs stand off, and the Korean and Vietnam wars, and concluded that these had all resulted from Group Think. Group Think led to a failure by the group to solve the problems effectively, as follows:

- The group discussed a minimum number of alternatives.
- The course of action favoured by the majority of members was not re-evaluated for hidden risks.
- Other alternative strategies were not considered.
- The group failed to use the expert opinions they had, and when expert opinion was evaluated it was done with a selective bias which ignored any facts and opinions which did not support the group view.

Other investigations into spectacular disasters such as the R101 airship disaster in the 1930s and the Challenger spaceship disaster found that both projects were led by groups suffering from Group Think and in situations where the perceived political consequences of not going ahead outweighed the perceived technical problems of proceeding.

In the voluntary sector, examples of Group Think might be:

- moving offices to a cheaper district, which most people find it more inconvenient to get to, but no one said anything prior to the move;
- ignoring the bad professional practices of one member of staff because the group would find it too hard to deal with disciplining them;
- introducing a performance-related pay scheme, against the advice of the personnel manager because the Chair of the Trustees wants one and no one has the nerve to say it won't work;
- no one being prepared to tell the Chief Executive to their face how out of step with the values of the rest of the organisation they are.

Antidotes to Group Think:

- The group leader or manager has to be willing to have their judgements criticised, and demonstrate that this is not only possible, but desirable.
- The group has to be willing to discuss doubts and minority views, and group members have to be prepared to voice them at the right time, not wallow in negativity behind people's backs.
- The opinion of experts, in whatever technical or management specialist field, must be valued and listened to properly – even if these 'experts' are actually the front-line workers who will have to put the decisions into effect.

## 4 Risky-shift phenomenon

It has been demonstrated that groups are willing to take greater risks than each individual would take if acting alone. The theory behind this is that the responsibility is perceived to be shared rather than shouldered alone.

Of course, it can sometimes happen that the group agrees to take on a new member of staff or to increase salaries without having the full facts at their disposal, or when a known 'dissenting' figure is absent.

The danger here is that when the full extent of the risk becomes known, all the relevant individuals deny being responsible for the original decision and therefore the risk, or they blame another person outside their original group for the failure. This is where the potential for conflict comes in.

Antidotes to 'Risky-shift':

- Ensure that all doubts are aired in the right arena before risky decisions are taken.
- Allocate levels of responsibility and authority within the group before risky decisions are taken.
- Always have the key information.

- Make sure all 'dissenters' are present for difficult decision-making.
- Never make long-term decisions for short-term reasons.

## 5  Groups and individuals

The interaction of groups and individuals has been a rich source of study for behavioural specialists. Individuals in teams are usually organised into groups in order to make the most of their mix of skills and abilities. However, too much emphasis on the group may subsume the individual contribution, whilst too much emphasis on the individual will make the development of the group less effective. Personal characteristics may also lead to conflict points.

'"A good team member" is an accolade the extraverts find easier to earn than introverts. Introverts have to work hard at it, learning and remembering to use the language of the team "we" rather than "I". Their high standards and their need for clarity and order often conflict with the extravert colleagues' way of doing things which to the introvert often seems slapdash and incomplete. The introvert, looking beyond the surface of things, will question what the team is doing, while the extravert, who is often prepared to complain to colleagues, will be less inclined to challenge the status quo.'

(Dorothy Rowe in *The Successful Self*, see *Further Reading*.)

The implications of this are that:

- individuals within groups can come to occupy certain roles or spaces or labels;
- individuals have a place in an invisible pecking order in teams;
- when individuals want to change their characteristics or display different ones, the group can sometimes resent this.

(See *Scenarios 1.3, 3.1, 4.1*.)

## 6 Team roles

Extensive research has shown that creating teams of people with similar skills and intelligence does not necessarily lead to effective performance. Meredith Belbin has made a study of the best mix of characteristics in a team, based upon research at Henley Management College. He also discovered that the team that looked the 'best' on paper did not necessarily perform the best. The characteristics outlined below will work best in a team, but that team may not necessarily get on well together. They will need to have good skills at dealing with differences in character and opinion. Most people have a natural preference for carrying out one or two different roles when working in teams. Belbin identified the inclusion of *co-ordinator* and *plant* roles as being particularly important.

As a manager it may be necessary to get other team members to appreciate the necessary skills that they all bring into the group, in order to allow the team to work to the best of its ability. For example, can you imagine the obvious conflicts that could result if a team had one 'shaper', one 'plant' and one 'company worker'? Managers can use these ideas to encourage staff to build on their strengths and not to take on roles that are not suited to their preferences. Also they can help staff reflect on skills that other team members have which are different from their own.

**The co-ordinator:** They organise the team and co-ordinate its efforts; they are disciplined, self-confident and balanced. They are a good communicator, a good judge of people and things, a person who works to motivate others. They hold the reins of the group together well.

**The team worker:** They also hold the team together, but in another way – by being supportive, listening to others, harmonising, encouraging, and understanding. Likeable and popular but uncompetitive, they are the sort of person you don't notice when they are there, but miss when they're not.

**The plant:** They are introverted, but intellectually dominant. The source of original ideas and proposals, being one of the most imaginative and intelligent of the group. They can be careless of details and may resent criticism. They need to be drawn out or they will switch off.

**The monitor–evaluator:** They are also intelligent, but in an analytic rather than a creative way. They carefully dissect ideas and see the flaws in arguments. They are dependable, often focussed on data, but can seem aloof and cold.

**The implementer:** The practical organiser. They turn ideas into manageable tasks. Schedules, charts and plans are their tools. Methodical, trustworthy and efficient, they are not excited by visions and can be unexciting themselves. Good administrators.

**The completer-finisher:** They check details, worry about schedules and chivvy the others with a sense of urgency. Relentless in their follow through, they are necessary but not always popular.

**The shaper:** Dominant, challenging and outgoing. The task leader – in the absence of the co-ordinator would leap into that role. They have drive and passion for the tasks, but can be over-sensitive, irritable and impatient. They challenge the team into action.

**The resource investigator:** The popular member, extrovert and resourceful. They bring new contacts, ideas and development to the group, the salesperson, diplomat or liaison officer. Not themselves original or a driver, they need the team to pick up their contribution.

**The specialist:** Dedicated individuals who pride themselves on acquiring technical skills and specialised knowledge. They maintain professional boundaries, show great pride in their own subject and little interest in other people's. They are single-minded, loners, dedicated and self-starting.

Too many of one role in a team means a lack of balance; too few roles and some tasks do not get done. In a small team, therefore, one person may have to perform more than one role. More stable groups can get by without all roles; but those in a rapidly changing environment or technology or product base need all functions. (See *Scenarios 4.1, 4.3*.)

(From *Management Teams*, see *Further Reading*. Also some paraphrasing from Charles Handy's descriptions of the team roles in *Understanding Organisations*.)

# 7 Victim / persecutor / rescuer

Here is a second way to look at the behaviour patterns that team members can acquire. The terms 'victim', 'persecutor', 'rescuer', are used to signify behaviours not people. There may be aspects of each role that are familiar – either in ourselves or in others. This triangle is a familiar pattern that can be observed working in some teams. Adopting one of these behaviour patterns will not help to encourage good conflict management. Any manager observing this pattern in themselves or their team needs to point it out and take action to deal with the negative aspects of the power triangle. Each individual might play out a bit of all behaviours from time to time.

The maintenance of this particular power triangle depends on the participation of all three roles. Each of the roles has its pay off, which is why participation in the triangle continues. Genuine victims of oppression are not included here. They need real support and will welcome possibilities of change. Someone taking a 'victim' role will commonly respond to all suggestions for change with 'Yes, but ...' One immediate response to this is to suggest that they try and say 'Yes, and ...'

# THE POWER GAME TRIANGLE

Persecutor                    Victim

Rescuer

## PERSECUTOR
*Bully*

**Says**
*'You won't, you mustn't, you will, you must, it's your fault'.*
Uses imperatives and orders. Language is full of blame and threat.
Presumes that the victim is always wrong and needs to be corrected.

**Pay offs**
Often gets what they want in the short term

**Drawbacks**
No basis for respect from others. Often has unsatisfactory relationships with people.

**Needs within the role**
To feel important and powerful.

## RESCUER
*Do-gooder*

**Says**
*'You can't, poor you, you shouldn't have to, you need my help'.*
Uses placatory words.
Language full of put downs towards the victim and admonitions towards the persecutor. Presumes that the victim is inadequate and incapable of self-help.

**Pay offs**
Manipulative power and control

**Drawbacks**
Insecurity of falling between two camps. Often afraid of losing friends.

**Needs within role**
To be liked by everyone.
To be indispensable to the lives of others.

## VICTIM
*Doormat*

**Says**
*'I can't, I'll fail, I don't know how, it's my fault, yes, but ...'*
Uses negatives and denials. Language full of dismissals and self pity.
Assumes inability to succeed or change.

**Pay off**
Others take responsibility.
No high expectations to live up to.

**Drawbacks**
Low self-esteem.
Powerlessness.

**Needs within role:**
To be looked after and to be cared for.

(From *Playing with Fire*, see *Further Reading*.)

## 8 Groups and boundaries

Until recently it has been unfashionable to talk of boundaries and what is involved in setting and sticking to them, whether in childcare, teaching or management. However, most people like boundaries. They want to know where they are and then they take action accordingly. If boundaries are not made explicit, then the team may find some members always pushing to find where the boundaries are. This may result in some outrageous behaviour before the limits can be established. It is not a sign of weakness for managers to set boundaries, but of strength – especially if they are set realistically and then adhered to.

- An unbounded group means trouble in the organisation and for group members.
- Hierarchies need to be explicit.
- Boundaries of group action within the hierarchy need to be made explicit.
- Boundaries of different groups or teams relating to each other need to be made explicit.

(See *Scenarios 1.1, 1.2, 2.1, 4.2, 5.*)

# Points of stress

Some common points of stress in a team where differences may be more exposed than usual or need re-capitulating are when:

- new individuals join;
- new team managers join;
- there is organisational change.

These are described in more detail in the scenarios in Part 2.

## 1 New members

When new team members join a team – and particularly in the case of a new team leader – the group norms and culture will be assessed and in some cases challenged. This may have the following consequences:

- group norms may be re-worked;
- the team may regress to an earlier stage of effectiveness;
- group norms and rules may need to be re-established.

For example:

- A new leader wants to change the way the team reports their absences or whereabouts.
- A new team member introduces doubts about the effectiveness of the current way of working.

- A team has to learn new groundrules in response to a newcomer making challenges to the attitudes of the group.

(See *Scenarios 1.1, 1.2.*)

## 2 Leadership

If there is a new group leader, their characteristics and management style will affect the effectiveness of the group and the likelihood of conflict. 'It is often with a sense of relief that the introvert becomes a team leader. "Now I can be myself and do things my way." This is not to say that all introverts make good leaders. They are often so taken up with their own ideas that they do not perceive the wishes and the needs of the people they manage. However, for the extravert, becoming a leader is a threat to the sense of self, and wise extraverts have to develop the necessary understanding and skills for leadership. The loneliness of command can seem to be like the isolation which extraverts fear as the threat to the sense of self.'

(Dorothy Rowe in *The Successful Self*. See *Further Reading*.)

Personal skills and management experience have an impact on the success of the new leader. There are usually high expectations on the part of the team and the new leader about their entrance into the organisation. The first few meetings might be ones where the leader is stretched or required to make some difficult intervention to 'show off' their management style, so that the existing team can get a better picture of who they are dealing with.

(See *Scenarios 1.1, 4.3, 5.*)

## 3 Organisational change

Times of change happen all too often in the voluntary sector, living as it does at the uncertain edge of funding. Where this change is fundamental to the organisation there are powerful forces at play. At a time when the continued success of the organisation may be at stake it is particularly important to facilitate good and careful discussion of all the options and to deal with conflicts successfully. This means:

- keeping communication as open and transparent as possible;
- ensuring that all options are considered – even 'way out' ones;
- helping main decision makers to be comfortable at expressing their opinions and feelings about what is going on;
- allowing all staff to have an opportunity to air opinions and feelings about the change.

(See *Scenarios 1.1, 5.*)

## 4 Badly managed team

One special challenge for managers is taking over a team or an organisation where the boundaries are not effective and behaviour has been let slip, or where a bully has gained control of the team. In this situation it is predictable that the manager's skills will be tested to the full and it is especially important to set boundaries and stick to them – even if they are over seemingly little issues such as filling in timesheets or expenses sheets.

## 5 Personal costs

In any situation behaviour may be influenced by perceived personal costs or risks. This applies particularly in responding to potentially violent situations, but also when the person thinks they may or may not be observed, or 'found out'. Harassment or bullying in these circumstances may happen.

People may also temper their behaviour if the conflict is with someone who is perceived to have more power over them. For example, although they may swear regularly with colleagues, they may not with the boss. They may habitually run from conflict, but not in a situation where someone else may be hurt or bullied.

(See *Scenarios 1.1, 1.3.*)

# Collectives

All of the above characteristics of groups and points of stress apply to collectives as well, plus a few extra ones including:

- hidden hierarchies
- the value of 'being a collective' overrides effectiveness
- no one to complain to
- feelings and resentments building up, with no legitimate safety valve
- fudging the ideas of management
- not taking decisions
- taking decisions over and over again.

# Organisational factors

Organisational factors may also affect the possibility of getting positive outcomes to conflicts.

- The office environment may itself be a cause of friction – either open plan or cubicle designs may be unsuitable; there may not be enough space, enough resources, etc.

- Hierarchies and reward systems may not be working or may be perceived to be not working for some staff or groups of staff.
- The organisation may be in a period of rapid growth or shrinking.
- What procedures are in place? For example, disciplinary or complaints procedures?

On top of personal factors, the organisational management culture may affect how we deal with conflict as an individual manager. For example the organisational culture may be of working long hours. While we do not have much control over that as an individual manager, it influences how we can operate effectively within that particular organisation. If some of the factors below combine, they can be the deciding elements in whether a manager can summon up the energy to handle conflict well. Or it may lead to the cumulative poor practice through lack of time to focus on staff or team issues. Other influences include:

- stress and institutionalised overwork;
- personal issues that are allowed to intrude at work inappropriately;
- lack of clarity, e.g. policies and procedures;
- lack of 'distance' between managers and staff;
- perceived threats, e.g. of redundancy or rivalry;
- a management culture of opposition and 'winning' at all costs.

## Management culture

Management culture is the pervading set of attitudes and beliefs in an organisation about how both resources and staff should be managed. In the most effective organisations it is explicit. It is discussed from time to time at a senior manager level and fed down by coaching or mentoring to line managers. Problems can arise when some aspects of management are not seen as important or recognised within an organisation. This can arise in the voluntary sector where organisations are very much led by service delivery and the goal might be expressed as to 'deliver the service at any cost'. In an organisation such as this:

- Managers may be skilled in service delivery or in planning budgets, but not necessarily in people skills or people management.
- The whole area of management as a process is not discussed.
- Typically there are few team meetings and differences are subsumed within the need to deliver.
- There may be a culture of overwork and a stress on the commitment to the organisation which is expressed solely in long hours.
- There may be unorthodox or unprofessional links between members of staff and the Management Committee.

(See *Unorthodox links to the Management Committee* in *Scenarios 1.1, 1.3.*)

Other issues may arise where:

- management is not understood as the same thing across the organisation;
- there are undefined boundaries between workers and clients or residents;
- there are no proper professional boundaries or policies;
- staff may work alone for a large part of the time and have little access to skilled supervision;
- attitudes to management vary – is a manager considered as one or more of these?

  a police person

  a hand-holder

  expected to wave a magic wand

  expected to carry out a 'mother' or a 'father' role

  expected to treat it as more than a job

  a special friend.

(See *Working alone* and *Lack of professional boundaries or training* in *Scenario 2.1.*)

| The are some management cultures in the voluntary sector that embody some archetypal responses to conflict: | |
|---|---|
| *laissez faire* | anything goes and there are no boundaries – or very unclear boundaries; |
| *divide and rule* | pitting team members or different teams against each other keeps them off my back; |
| *trigger happy* | 'a good disciplinary never hurt anyone'; or letting poor performance go unchecked or unchallenged until one day the employee finds a final written warning on their desk; |
| *personality cult* | 'Susan would say that, wouldn't she?' Either blame or scapegoating one individual. Or letting a person off the hook because of some endearing personality trait. |
| *head in the sand* | 'Conflict? What conflict?' |
| *paterfamilial* | 'We're one big (happy?) family here.' But whose family are we talking about? |
| *The Emperor's got no clothes* | 'You tell him – no you tell him!' |

(See *Managerial culture* in *Scenarios 1.1, 1.2, 4.1, 4.2.*)

Unfortunately it is beyond the scope of this book to describe further the characteristics and effects of these cultures. Other sources are *Just about Managing* and *Understanding Voluntary Organisations*. (See *Further Reading*.)

## Role models, skills and confidence

If a manager is not inherently confident at dealing with conflict at work, managerial skills may be increased by observing role models. If the manager has had poor role models this will increase their likely failures as conflict resolvers.

One central feature of mentoring, coaching or management training should be how to deal effectively with team differences and conflicts.

# PERSONAL RESPONSES TO CONFLICT

## Introduction

While Chapter 3 covered managerial and organisational influences on the way we handle conflict as a manager and as an individual, Chapter 4 looks at personal responses to conflict. This chapter will be of use to managers who want either to think through their own responses at an emotional as well as analytical level, or to gain an insight into others' responses they find puzzling or hard to understand. It will also be of use to any individual employee involved in conflict wishing to think through their reactions.

Most employees do not change personal styles or communication patterns as soon as they step over the threshold of the workplace. They bring with them the same skills and abilities in interpersonal relationships that they use in other areas of their lives. Among those are how they react to difference and any techniques they have developed for dealing with it and their approach to conflict. To become a better and calmer conflict resolver it is essential to be more aware of one's own and other's patterns in dealing with it and to be aware of learned responses to difficult situations that may need challenging or reshaping to get the best results.

Many people assume that dealing with conflict is an inbuilt skill that everyone can be effective at, like communication. But communication skills aren't equally distributed either. Some people also have an attitude that their way of solving problems is the only way and can't be changed. 'Leopards can't change their spots', they say. This could well be a smokescreen for a variety of different reactions. For a manager confronting this sort of response, it will be appropriate to explore it in detail to find the most appropriate route to achieve change. The 'real' message could be:

'I don't see why I should change and I'm not going to anyway. You can't make me.'

'Just because I work here doesn't mean I have to behave in a different way from my normal one.'

'I might recognise that I need to change, but I'm not going to say that in front of my colleagues'.

'I want to change, but don't know how.'

For those who want to change but don't know how, the good news is that there are skills and techniques that can be learned to increase your ability to both analyse and manage conflict. However, to get the best out of them implies spending time looking at how you prefer to handle conflict now.

# How do I handle conflict now?

Once you have begun to analyse conflicts you realise that there are many variables affecting the chance of a positive outcome. In some cases there will be nothing that can be done to influence that outcome, whether because of organisational circumstances or the indifference of the other parties. However, in some cases personal skills and experience can make a significant difference. This chapter offers suggestions for analysing our instinctive or natural approach to conflict.

Each person has a learnt set of skills for handling conflict: their *pattern*. Unfortunately, given the pervasive negativity about dealing with conflict in the UK, these may not be the best ones. However, the good news is that they can be improved on.

*For example:* 'For many years I always reacted to any challenge or conflict that involved anger with the gut reaction that this was somehow my fault, rather than looking at why the other person was angry. This led me to avoid conflict and to be nervous around people who seemed to operate at a challenging level the whole time. I still have a shadow of this response – but I am learning to move beyond my learnt pattern.'

To begin the process of self analysis let's look at what factors in someone's style or history might lead them towards a negative or less than assertive response in a conflict situation.

## Factors contributing to a negative outcome

Every person has an inherent style in handling conflict that has been learned over the years. Some factors in this style in themselves make a negative outcome more likely. For example, the list below contains sample suggestions from a managing conflict training course in response to the question: 'How do I handle conflict now?'. It is a single list in no order of importance.

| | |
|---|---|
| My ability not appreciated | The other person dismisses things |
| I get scared and close down | which are important to me |
| I come over as unapproachable | Stress |
| I have fixed ideas and am not | I feel out of the clique |
| willing to shift | I feel anger and bitterness |

| | |
|---|---|
| I do not trust the other person | I leave without resolving matters |
| If I feel I'm not being listened to | I want revenge |
| My style is not compatible with others | I feel there is injustice |
| | I am the problem |
| I feel disrespected | I don't communicate my feelings effectively |
| People not talking directly to me about things that concern me | |
| | I allow resentment to build up |
| Feeling they are putting me down | My pride |
| They show off | My stubbornness |
| I feel misunderstood | Personality clash |
| They are not listening to me | |

Feelings that may contribute to negative conflict outcomes:

- overpowered
- out of control – unable to alter the situation (forced or compelled)
- taken for granted – unappreciated – minimised
- guilty
- dependent on authority
- inferior – inadequate in a given situation
- rejected – being disliked or unacceptable
- insensitively treated
- unheard or misunderstood
- manipulated – not being informed or privy to important information
- uninvolved in problem-solving issues that affect daily lives.

# Where does our personal pattern come from?

There are many different components involved in the development of our preferred pattern of response to conflict. The most influential of these are:

*Set 1*
- inherent personality traits
- role models, including family
- beliefs and attitudes – our culture

*Set 2*
- any 'label' we may have
- any 'head messages' or regular fears and fantasies

Set 3
- our power in any situation
- the perceived cost of acting in a certain way in that situation

An individual may be heavily influenced by any or all of the above. The first set of factors leads to a more ingrained pattern of response, which may become almost instinctive. The second set may reflect a deep pattern of behaviour or may have a varying effect on outcomes depending upon the relative importance of the factor in a specific situation. The third set may influence actions taken in that particular workplace or with certain staff or in certain circumstances.

## 1 Inherent personality traits

There are several ways of describing inherent traits: one is to look at preferred ways of connecting – some people are primarily visual, some verbal, some prefer the written word.

### Introvert/extravert

Dorothy Rowe in *The Successful Self* makes a distinction between introvert and extravert, which is rather different from our everyday use of the words. She adapts definitions of the types from Jung's work on psychoanalysis.

**Extravert:** experiencing your existence as a member of a group, as the relationship, the connection between yourself and others.

Extraverts see the threat of annihilation of the self as complete isolation, being left totally, utterly and forever alone, fading away, totally disappearing into nothingness.

Extraverts can make themselves members of a group in a wide variety of ways – large family, large number of friends, members of teams, run a business with colleagues, enter one of the helping professions. If an extravert has had an early bad experience with people, they may still gather 'friends' around them in the form of pets, books, heroes and heroines from fantasy.

**Introvert:** Experiencing existence as the progressive development of individuality in terms of clarity, achievement and authenticity.

Introverts see the threat of annihilation of the self as losing control of yourself and falling apart, falling into chaos, fragmenting and crumbling to dust.

Where an introvert works with an extravert and neither of them is tolerant of the other's inherent preferences or style, this could be an underlying cause of tension.

## 2 My family and other role models

The earliest environment for dealing with conflict is the family setting. Here each person struggles to gain a sense of themselves in relation to adults and any siblings. Early relationships with adults may influence our attitude to authority in later life and relationships with siblings will affect our sense of rivalry with colleagues.

Adults who are skilled and insightful can show us the way to relate successfully to adults as authority figures, and how to build bridges with siblings in order to learn that each person has something of value to offer the world. Or the adults may not be skilled and insightful and may not help in dealing with conflicts and emotions that arise in childhood. In these situations the child may learn survival mechanisms that help in these early years, but they may not be the most useful skills for dealing with conflict in adult life.

Since no one's upbringing is 'perfect', it is highly likely that you will recognise some of these traits or patterns you have learned in childhood:

hiding emotions
fear of anger
bursting with inappropriate anger
not being able to name emotions
bullying behaviour
victim behaviour
passive or aggressive behaviour
inappropriate competitiveness
manipulative behaviour
reacting inappropriately to people who remind us of our parents or siblings

Other significant adults in our lives – teachers, friends, etc. – can give us different examples of behaviour and models. Later on in life, other colleagues and managers can be role models for good practice.

**It is not the aim of this book to be a psychology text** – there are plenty of others. The *Further Reading* section has some starting points for anyone concerned to explore these matters.

## 3 Cultural differences

An additional layer that may influence how we act in a team involves cultural differences. Some differences between two individuals are immediately visible, but there are also those that are not apparent at first yet may impact strongly on how a person behaves in a team or reacts in a conflict situation. It is appealing to look for the sameness in others and to be reassured by it – yet it is the differences we are concerned with here. The iceberg image below helps us to think of the hidden and dangerous nature of assuming sameness, where none may exist.

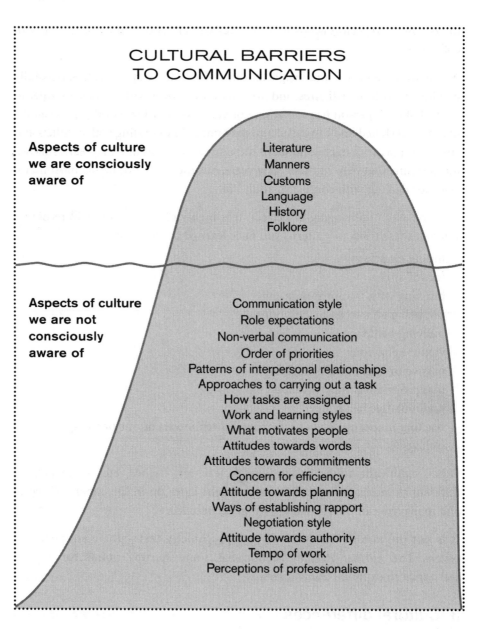

CULTURAL BARRIERS
TO COMMUNICATION

Aspects of culture
we are consciously
aware of

Literature
Manners
Customs
Language
History
Folklore

Aspects of culture
we are not
consciously
aware of

Communication style
Role expectations
Non-verbal communication
Order of priorities
Patterns of interpersonal relationships
Approaches to carrying out a task
How tasks are assigned
Work and learning styles
What motivates people
Attitudes towards words
Attitudes towards commitments
Concern for efficiency
Attitude towards planning
Ways of establishing rapport
Negotiation style
Attitude towards authority
Tempo of work
Perceptions of professionalism

## 4 My label

Human nature tends to categorise people. We give labels to ourselves and others give labels to us. For example: strong, unhappy, moody, feminist, direct, bossy. This can then influence other experiences even if they are potentially contradictory to the label. The label is the first impression, whether the person is acting in that way or not. For example if a person is known as 'stuffy', they will be seen as acting out of character even if they tell the wittiest jokes in the office and become the informal social secretary. We may come to resent a label that determines expectations about our responses.

## 5 'Head messages'

I use the phrase 'head messages' to refer to the conversations that happen in our own heads in certain situations. For example, there may be a particular difficulty with someone at work or we may want to prepare for a conversation with the residents about something we fear might involve conflict. In this situation it is tempting to run a 'scenario' to prepare for the event. However, where this means putting words into other people's mouths, it can be frustrating to realise that they don't respond in the way the fantasy says they will. Once they start moving away from 'our' script, the whole scenario is ruined. This can mean that the person originating the script can no longer behave spontaneously. Preparing for a potentially difficult situation is wise, but not to the extent of writing the script for the other participants.

## 6 My power

In situations that people find difficult, they are likely to fall back on any power, either personal or organisational, available to them. For a manager, this power may be legitimate, but you need to be careful to set legitimate boundaries for expressing it and not be tempted to use it unfairly or oppressively. Some examples where power can be exercised inappropriately are:

- to give rewards or withhold them unfairly or against procedures;
- to coerce workers into behaviour patterns acceptable to the manager and to discipline for unacceptable behaviour;
- to discriminate on the basis of gender, race, sexuality, level of ability, or people's characteristics;
- as a colleague, to withhold information, not to pass messages on.

# My normal response

So how does all the above add up to normal behaviour in relation to any conflict? What do I normally do – how does this affect what is going on? Do I wade in or opt out? Do I get a buzz out of a row or does it make me feel sick? If you want to try putting all your personal factors together, see the charts – including a completed example – in the *Appendix*.

chapter ⑤

# TECHNIQUES FOR HANDLING CONFLICT

## What's going on?
## Techniques for conflict diagnosis

### Step 1

Asking *What's going on?* in an analytical way is often the key to a manager's or individual's ability to manage conflict constructively. A clear understanding of the differences between the concerns or perspectives of the two parties, and the sources of those differences, is important. This means stopping and asking:

'What's going on?'

The key questions that follow on are:

'What is the nature of the differences in this conflict?'
'What is the reason for the differences?'

Some examples of answers to those questions follow. Once you are clear about the nature and reason for the differences underlying the conflict, then you can take the first step in appropriate action to deal with them.

### Nature of differences

**Facts:** the present situation, the present problem
*There is / There isn't enough money in the budget.*
*There are 450 clients per month. / There are 350 per month.*
**Goals:** how things ought to be
*We need a new drop-in centre. / We need more residential units.*
*We need a new computer. / We need an information strategy.*
**Methods:** the best route to follow
*Campaigning will get results. / Campaigning will alienate our traditional supporters.*
*We need a mailing. / We need to canvas support on the doorstep.*

**Values:** the long-range beliefs about what priorities should be observed in choosing goals and methods.

*We must apply to the Lottery. / We can't take money from gambling.*

*A collective way of working is the only truly democratic way to organise. / Collectives allow too much scope for timewasters without enough responsibility.*

## Reasons for differences

Among the most common are:

**Information** The two parties have been exposed to different information and so have arrived at a different understanding of what the problem or issue is.

**Perception** Sometimes people have been exposed to the same data, but their past experience causes them to interpret it in different ways.

**Role** Sometimes people's roles cause them to take different positions. They do not look at the same data or perceive them in the same way, and they may advocate different goals.

**Values** Sometimes people's value systems lead to different goals being sought or different methods preferred.

## Other possible factors

**Personality** Pessimistic/optimistic; cautious/risk taking; brisk/needs time to think things through

**Attitude/Prejudice** The sort of undermining messages such as 'Women are not competent finance managers'; 'Gay people should not be 'out' 'at work'; 'The dreadlocks distract me from the skills'.

**Communication style** Direct/indirect; succinct/rambling; planned/tangential.

**Culture** For example: Being direct is impolite; organising behind the manager's back is just covering my own; borrowing from petty cash on Friday is fine.

(The above lists have been expanded from 'Handling Conflict' in From *Strength to Strength*, see *Further Reading*.)

# Step 2

What are the individual people bringing to the conflict in communication pattern / personal style?

# Step 3

Are there any team factors to be taken into account?

## Step 4

Are there any organisational factors to be taken into account?

## Step 5

If there are, does this involve other key people that I need to take account of in resolving the conflict?

## Step 6

Does the difference involve harassment, bullying or breaking the organisation's code of conduct? Should I go straight to the Disciplinary procedure?

# Toolkit for managers

The different roles that can be taken in conflict resolution fall into five broad groups.

1   Unequal participant in a conflict because of power imbalances – for example a manager in conflict with an employee. (See *Scenarios 1.2, 1.3, 1.4.*)
2   Intervenor in conflict between two or more others where the parties may not seek or want a solution immediately. (See *Scenario 2.2.*)
3   Neutral mediator between two or more parties seeking a solution voluntarily. (See *Scenarios 1.3, 2.2.*)
4   Team facilitator – being an outsider for the team in conflict. (See *Scenarios 3.1, 5.*)
5   Equal participant in a conflict. (See *Scenarios 4.1, 4.2, 4.3.*)

The contribution that an individual can make to resolving a conflict will obviously depend on their role. In addition, different techniques are going to be appropriate at different times and for different reasons. The desire to get a positive outcome is also important.

## Manager and employee

As a manager there are two main options:

■ management action short of the disciplinary procedure;
■ disciplinary action (see section at the end of this chapter).

Harassment, violence and bullying are extreme examples of conflict. Although it may well fall to a manager to deal with them, the techniques and issues are somewhat different, so these are covered in separate sections. (See sections on *Harassment* and *Bullying* at the end of this chapter.)

## Management action short of the disciplinary procedure

The critical path approach to management action is as follows:

1   Think through your perception of the:
    nature of the differences;
    reason for the differences.
2   Think through the models in Chapter 2 (whichever seems most appropriate) for clues to behaviour of the employee.
3   Think through what you know of the employee in other settings.
4   Does it involve possible prejudiced behaviour? If yes, go to 8.
    Throughout this thinking process stay as objective as possible.
5   Check out your initial conclusions with the employee.
6   Give more information or get more information.
7   Suggest a solution and take an interim decision if all relevant factors seem dealt with.
    If this does not resolve the situation, other factors that are not yet exposed may be in operation.
8   Explore other issues to do with the employee and their personal attitudes to conflict.
9   Explore other issues to do with organisational or team factors.
10   Set or re-set boundaries as appropriate.
11   Bring in extra authority, if they are not responding to your authority – discuss with your own manager or other mentor.
12   Take clear decisions and monitor subsequent events.
13   Record any expected changes in behaviour or team rules or organisational rules.
14   Use the disciplinary procedure if the response to the above is inadequate.
15   Possibly use outside consultants to show up organisational problems.
16   Possibly use team facilitation if the underlying issues involve team dynamics that need exposing – but this is best not done by you.

Some of these steps could happen in a policy meeting, individual meetings, team meetings, supervision or special meetings to expose and resolve conflicts. If it seems that the situation is getting out of control or beyond your resources to deal with, then talk to a senior manager sooner rather than later. (See *Scenarios 1.1, 4.2.*)

# Intervenor

Intervention is not a neutral tool. It involves taking direct action to put yourself at the heart of a conflict where you see that it is counterproductive to let it continue. Good intervention allows both parties to keep their dignity, does not blame or scapegoat one side, but attempts to safeguard parties from harm, physical or psychological. It helps people learn from the encounter and empowers individuals to be able to solve their own conflicts more creatively and with more positive outcomes in future. This technique might also be useful for employees intervening in conflicts between residents or users. Suggestions here are always superseded if violence is an issue. If the person feels that there is a likelihood of violence, then they should follow the organisation's health and safety rules. Any staff that might be at risk of violence from the public or clients should be given appropriate specialist training in diffusing violence and keeping themselves safe.

The most skilled interventions involve a process of modelling good conflict resolution techniques.

Sample steps in intervention:

1   Notice what is going on and act appropriately. This may mean repeating a simple phrase to gain the attention of the participants who may be shouting at each other (the 'broken record' technique). Use a succinct form of words, such as:

    'Calm down'; 'Don't shout'; 'I want you to stop'.

    And keep repeating until they run out of steam. If one is shouting at the other, address your words loudly but calmly at them.

2   Separate the parties to allow a cooling off.

3   Talk to each party separately in neutral terms about what was happening. Do not collude in blaming or in any oppression that may be happening at this point.

4   Try and bring each person to an understanding of the nature of the differences between them and what they would like to see as a solution.

5   If both are willing, bring them together to facilitate a reconciliation and a solution that both find acceptable.

6   Always keep the parameters within the organisation's rules and procedures.

7   It may need more than one intervention to enable people to be able to hear each other and work together comfortably.

The key elements of any intervention are

Try and model good resolution skills.
Notice unacceptable behaviour.
Encourage learning not blame.
Strong feelings are OK – abuse isn't.

Ideas for words or phrases that can be helpful in calming down an ugly conflict between two other people.

'What is going on?'

'Am I missing something?'

'I can see you're heated, but ...?'

'I don't think that it is OK to ...' or 'It is not appropriate to ...'

'I don't understand.'

'Do you mean that ...?'

'I can hear that you're angry, but the way you're dealing with it is damaging the other person.'

'Shouting is not OK.'

*reflecting*

'You seem ...'

*checking out*

'Are you saying that ... ?'

*buying time*

'That's an interesting idea.'

### Golden rules for making interventions in conflict

- Notice what's going on.
- Name it and check it out.
- Use 'broken record' technique if appropriate.
- Ask what's going on.
- Strong emotion is OK, damage isn't.
- Acknowledge what is going on.
- Mirror and reflect back.
- Know and hold the organisation's rules and boundaries.
- Aim to empower others to deal with their own conflict issues.

(See *Scenario 2.2.*)

## Neutral mediator

Mediation is not always an appropriate tool to try in the workplace and should not be offered if a process which does not involve outside intervention is more appropriate as a first step. Mediation is a neutral tool. It provides an opportunity for both parties to explore the nature of their differences and to come to a mutually agreed position. In some circumstances it requires very sensitively trained mediators: for example those who model any differences that are at the heart of a conflict, such as white – black; male – female; straight – gay, etc.

Mediators are trained to listen to those in conflict and to help them resolve their disagreements. A mediator is not giving advice nor acting as a referee or as a manager for the purposes of the mediation. Mediators aim to facilitate a reconciliation by creating both space and a supportive framework within which those in dispute can resolve their difficulty themselves and take ownership of the solution.

Conditions for mediation:

- The parties must agree that a resolution is needed.
- Mediation is 'without prejudice', i.e. parties can reserve the right to invoke other measures.
- The parties must have the authority to settle.
- Any agreements have to be to the satisfaction of the parties concerned.
- The content of the mediation is confidential to the parties. Any agreement may need to be seen by the manager in this type of dispute – but the process might simply be about exploring differences, in which case no notes need to be seen.
- The mediator is neutral and impartial and has to be seen as such throughout the proceedings.
- The process is voluntary.

Andrew Acland in *A Sudden Outbreak of Common Sense* (see *Further Reading*) suggests that the circumstances *favouring mediation* are that:

- relationships are important;
- those involved want to retain control of the outcome;
- both sides have a good cause;
- there is not great disparity in power;
- speed is important;
- confidentiality is important;
- both sides need the opportunity to let off steam;
- neither side really wants to use the disciplinary procedure.

In some organisations or teams difficult situations can arise that are not appropriate to resolve through the disciplinary or disputes procedure. In this case, involving a mediator may be a creative and helpful way forward. All the previous points need to be taken into account in deciding whether this is an appropriate tool to use.

If your organisation is big enough to have different departments it might be possible to train in-house mediators to be involved in disputes in other parts of the organisation. This will only be appropriate where they have complete neutrality. Given the internal politics in most organisations, this may be unlikely. Getting a mediator in from outside may look expensive, but it could help resolve a difficult situation more quickly and completely than would otherwise be possible. It costs no more than getting an external team supervisor or facilitator.

> **What does a workplace mediation process involve?**
> Two or more parties identify that there is a 'problem'.
> A manager identifies that mediation would be the appropriate resolution tool.
> The parties agree to undertake mediation.
> A trained mediator is approached.
> A date and a neutral setting is arranged – allow half a day at least.
> The mediator(s) open the meeting with all parties, to agree ground-rules and make introductions.
> Each side opens with how they see the issue – no comments or questions from the other side at this point.
> The mediator(s) work through the issues either face to face or shuttling from separate room to separate room.
> As any agreements are reached by the participants, they are agreed with all parties involved.
> A formal record will be made at the conclusion of the mediation.
> A review meeting may be held at an agreed time after the mediation, to monitor progress on the agreements.

In commercial and community mediation it has been shown that 90% of people who agree to mediate reach an agreement.

The National Council for Voluntary Organisations (NCVO) and Centre for Dispute Resolution (CEDR) set up a joint mediation service targeted at the voluntary sector in 1998. The service provides trained mediators – all are CEDR accredited – and is subsidised. Mediation UK can also provide information on mediators in your area (see *Resources*). Trained mediators with voluntary sector experience are available from the above NCVO/CEDR mediation service, via some local Councils for Voluntary service and from some consultants specialising in mediation and managing conflict work (see *Resources*).

## Outside facilitator

In some circumstances it may be beneficial to involve an outsider in team processes. However the team must always work with a clear understanding and expectations of the process. Outside facilitators are not able to act as line mangers or as a substitute for internal processes or to provide a panacea for all team problems.

Strategies for any team to improve the way it deals with conflict must:

- build trust;
- build on the strengths of individuals in the team;
- increase the accuracy of communication;
- ensure the individual members of the group are working for the same ends in the team.

Techniques that can be used are:

- list and chart previous conflicts and their outcomes in order to make clear any patterns that are going on and expose differences in perceptions among team members;
- chart unresolved conflicts;
- list different techniques for resolving conflicts;
- role play alternative and more productive conflict coping strategies;
- draw out each individual's place in the team.

In all cases this should be done by a skilled facilitator, either from within the organisation, but in a respected position and trained in facilitation, or a trained outside facilitator.

If you do want to use a facilitator there are two main sources apart from your own local knowledge. NCVO produce a directory of management consultants working with the voluntary sector. Management Development Network is an association of management consultants working predominantly with the voluntary sector. They produce a guide to their members. (See *Resources*.)

Among keys to success in using an outside facilitator are:

- Define clearly the outcomes you are looking for from their involvement.
- Do not expect a quick fix solution to deep-rooted and long-standing problems.
- Check they have the skills and knowledge to do the job.
- Always ask for detailed references from previous clients.
- Make sure that you can work with them – some people's style may just not suit your organisation.
- Always have a written contract with them specifying any deadlines and exactly what you are paying for.

## Techniques for individuals

The assumption made here is that the participants are relatively equal in power terms in the organisation.

When you are entering into a potential conflict situation it is wise to be prepared – to know what you will compromise on and what you won't. If situations are 'sprung' on you, take time to think if necessary. You could also comment on the unfortunate timing and suggest a discussion at a later stage when you have had time to think.

Prepare:

- Think through your position.
- Think through statements and make sure they are couched in language that is not inflammatory or potentially offensive.

First phase:

- Ask for clarification.
- Paraphrase the other's position to make sure you have understood it.
- Don't make assumptions about the other's position or reasons for it – ask!
- Create space.

Second phase:

- Take time to think if you feel you need it.
- Acknowledge your emotions and theirs.
- Don't demonise or scapegoat.
- Separate the behaviour from the person.
- Be proactive and don't prevaricate.
- Be informed and know procedures.
- Confront untruths and be honest yourself.

Ending:

- Check both parties' understanding of the outcomes.
- Ensure a clear deadline is set if appropriate.

> ### Skills needed to be a good resolver of conflicts
>
> Awareness of people's different styles, patterns of communication and cultures.
>
> Ability to handle feelings in self and others in a way that doesn't deny their power or existence.
>
> Awareness of one's own pattern of conflict resolution.

Ability to analyse what is going on in each conflict that is encountered.

Ability to suggest solutions that stimulate participants to think further for themselves.

Ability to listen carefully and communicate effectively and assertively at any given interaction.

Sense of equality and an awareness of potential reticences in communication.

## Communication techniques

Here is a brief list of practical ideas for what you can do to strengthen these communication skills commonly used in resolving conflicts.

| **Neutral questions establishing facts** | NOT |
|---|---|
| 'Did you miss the deadline?' | 'You missed the deadline again!' |
| 'Did Tom give you instructions?' | 'Did you stop to think of the consequences of your stupid action?' |
| | 'Why didn't you follow Tom's instructions?' |
| | 'Why did you ignore Tom?' |
| **Focus on the issues not the personalities** | |
| 'We are here to sort out the communication issues over management team meetings.' | 'Susan forgot the mailing again.' |
| | 'Jeff failed to meet the deadline.' |
| | 'Frances didn't tell me the right date.' |
| **Express yourself in 'I' messages** | |
| 'I want to work this out.' | 'It's important to work this out.' |
| 'I am unhappy with your response.' | 'Your response is not good enough.' |
| 'I think that the accounts format needs revision.' | 'The accounts must be revised.' |

## Dealing with harassment and prejudiced behaviour

A different approach is appropriate to conflict between colleagues where one of the individuals is exhibiting anti-social behaviour or lacking awareness about appropriate language, behaviour or actions. Some people might say that dealing with behaviour of this nature always has to be a disciplinary issue. However, sometimes the offended party may prefer it to be looked at informally to begin with. This has to be their choice.

(See *Scenario 1.3.*)

## The definition of harassment

Harassment is deliberate unacceptable behaviour which is unreasonable, unwelcome or offensive. It might be physical, verbal or non-verbal, and might be directed against an individual or arise in a gathering such as a meeting, public event or party. Harassment should always be dealt with under the disciplinary procedure.

Harassment on any basis, not only race or sex, may fall within the criminal offence of intentional harassment, if it involves harassment, alarm or distress caused by threatening, abusive or insulting words or behaviour, disorderly behaviour, or writing, signs or other visible representations which are threatening, abusive or insulting (Criminal Justice and Public Order Act 1994). The Commission of Racial Equality code has advice on racial harassment. The Department for Education and Employment has a booklet on sexual harassment in the workplace based on the European Union's Code on the Dignity of Women and Men at Work. These codes, and decisions at Employment Appeal Tribunal level in harassment cases emphasise the importance of:

- having proper procedures to deal with claims;
- informing employees of what behaviour constitutes harassment;
- taking action if you know harassment is going on.

The **Protection from Harassment Act 1997** is not specifically aimed at the employment situation, but does make it a criminal offence for an individual to pursue a course of action which amounts to harassment and which they know is harassment. Harassment is defined as 'alarming the other person or causing the person distress' and a 'course of action' must involve at least two occasions. The Act also makes it a criminal offence to cause someone fear that an act of violence will be done against them.

Harassment can take a variety of forms, from a violent abusive attack to the 'dripping tap' accumulation of intrusions. People may be ignored, left out of the process of consultation or treated differently from the other workers in a subtle manner. The difficulty of defining and categorising harassment is precisely what deters people from reporting it or complaining of behaviour which causes distress. They run the risk of not being believed or of having their experiences trivialised or being accused of 'provoking' it.

No one invites or provokes harassment. To suggest that people deliberately invite insulting behaviour is the main way in which the harassers use their power position in the established oppressive order to justify their behaviour.

## Developing a policy

The first act of any organisation should be to develop a policy on harassment covering racial harassment, sexual harassment, heterosexual harassment and harassment on any other discriminatory ground. This is vital. By doing nothing, management and individuals are tacitly supporting those who harass. It is essential to protect people from the consequences of harassment because:

- harassment tends to get worse if it is not dealt with;
- it is a major contributor to stress at work;
- it causes absenteeism and staff turnover which reflects badly on the employment record of the person affected;
- without policies, those who complain run the risk of facing retaliation and possible loss of their job.

The management needs to draw up a statement and policy in consultation with staff, develop a training programme on dealing with harassment, and develop procedures for dealing with grievances and disciplinary action. Procedures for dealing with any complaint of harassment must take as the starting point that the person complaining is believed. Never dismiss any complaint as unreasonable because you do not regard it as harassment – the point is that the person complaining does regard it as such.

For the system to work, people need to have confidence in it – confidence that the policy and procedures have been developed in order to deal with the problem, not as a cosmetic exercise. A deterrent to using these policies can arise if the complainant rather than the harasser is treated as the 'problem' employee. Unfortunately this often happens, because management are unsure of the issues, not trained to deal with harassment and would rather the issue didn't exist. For example, in one organisation, line managers failed to support staff who had frequently complained about the Finance Director. Complaints about his appalling attitudes, bad manners and foul language were repeatedly dismissed. Over a period of 12 months, 14 previously valued and respected staff either faced instant dismissal or handed in their notice, simply to escape his reign of terror.

## Dealing with a complaint

The first step is to find out exactly what happened and listen to the person's complaint from beginning to end.

The second step is to explain the policy on harassment and sort out the most appropriate action. Make a record of the interview and keep it confidential. Then take the action decided upon quickly. This could be formal or informal. Any delay at this stage is very serious as it is unacceptable for the person to have to continue working with the harasser unless they know that their complaint is being taken seriously and that action will be taken.

## Informal stage

An informal approach, if managed well, may have more chance of changing behaviour than disciplinary penalties – but only if it is not used to cover up any discrimination issues involved in the conflict. If the complainant would prefer an informal approach first, then one plan of action might be:

- set up an initial meeting with both parties, separately;
- ask neutral questions first, to assess the position of the person accused of harassment;
- listen to the person, but don't collude in or give approval to any slanted or prejudiced remarks or comments;
- ask challenging questions to make sure you understand their internal dynamic;
- agree a course of action that can be monitored at the end and make plain that further infringements could lead to the formal disciplinary measures;
- inform the complainant of the outcome.

This technique has its limitations depending on the response that you get. If the person is unwilling or not able to respond to this kind of interaction, then the disciplinary procedure is going to be more appropriate. The manager will need to monitor all actions very carefully. If the complainant is not satisfied with the level of behaviour change, they should have the right to complain again and to suggest the disciplinary course of action the second time, rather than trying again informally. To be able to facilitate such a process, you will also need to be skilled in the following:

- being aware of diversity issues and actively involved in challenging yourself;
- being assertive;
- phrasing neutral and challenging questions;
- active listening.

John Crawley in his book, *Constructive Conflict Management,* goes through in detail some useful examples of actual words and phrases that can be used in this and other types of conflicts (see *Further Reading*).

## Formal Stage

If the complaint cannot be resolved informally, then ensure as far as possible that the grievance is investigated by someone independent of the department to which the grievance relates, who has been trained to understand how discrimination and harassment take place and the hurt they can cause.

- Ensure that the policy requires management to respond within a fixed time limit (not more than two weeks) and the grievance is settled as quickly as is practicable.
- Make it clear that discrimination and harassment are disciplinary offences, the penalty for which may include dismissal.

- Communicate the outcome of the grievance, including any disciplinary action taken against the offender, to the complainant with a written undertaking that they will not be victimised or suffer any other detriment.

## Dealing with bullying

A recent survey by the University of Stafford found that 78% of people thought they had witnessed bullying at work and 51% had experienced it. Overworked and stressed managers are replacing managers with difficult personalities as the main culprits in workplace bullying, according to an employer- and union-sponsored survey conducted in December 1998. The first nation-wide survey of its kind undertaken by Manchester University and the CBI and TUC follows a string of recent research showing that bullying and abuse at work is becoming more widespread. The TUC estimates that 5 million people have been bullied at work. (See *Scenario 1.1, 1.4, 3.2.*)

Andrea Adams, in her book *Bullying at work* (see *Further Reading*), defines it as:
'The persistent demeaning and downgrading of human beings through vicious words, cruel unseen acts which gradually undermines their confidence and self-esteem.'

The power of the bully is often to silence others through fear. Even where there is a grievance procedure staff may be too frightened to use it. So organisations must adopt a clear strategy.

There are different types of bullying and many grievances may seem trivial, but added together they become a psychological catalogue of horrors. For example:

**Managerial:** replacing responsibility with menial tasks; changing the boundaries of workplace responsibility half way through a task deliberately to intimidate; unconstructive criticism.

**Emotional:** excluding (not talking to, not including in discussions); ridicule (being told you are stupid, inefficient, not making the correct decision professionally); humiliation in front of other staff, pressure in staff meetings, constant questioning.

**Verbal:** shouting, rudeness, yelling, screaming, sarcasm; spreading rumours; questioning a person's sanity when they do not react as expected or as wanted; reacting to a minor problem or issue with the same vehemence as a major one. Whilst each one of these instances might seem trivial, the long-term cumulative effect can be devastating.

People bully for many reasons. They may feel insecure or stressed, or they may just never have learned a better way. Whatever the reason their managerial behaviour needs changing. A bullying manager may:

- consider they are never wrong;

- blame everyone but themselves;
- be poor at communicating;
- be prone to anger and irritability;
- be charming to seniors and outsiders, but tyrannical to subordinates;
- be vindictive;
- need to control;
- be good at twisting the truth.

Other managers and senior managers need to be aware of these potential signs of poor management practice.

## Policies

It is important to ensure that policies or codes of conduct refer explicitly to bullying. Staff should treat each other with dignity and respect, and behaviour which is demeaning, demoralising, intimidating or unfair should be treated as harassment. A complaint should always be taken seriously. Many employees feel they will not be believed and will hesitate to bring up issues or complaints which may on their own seem trivial. Using the formal grievance procedure may be the only way to stop persistent bullying.

Managers can confront the problem by:

- making it clear to employees that they recognise bullying as a problem;
- identifying what is reasonable behaviour and establishing disciplinary procedures for unreasonable actions;
- ensuring that job descriptions are secure and unequivocal;
- believing staff when they complain of bullying, and supporting them through the investigation and disciplinary process;
- getting evidence;
- reassuring the bullied that they can't be further intimidated;
- discussing problems with the bully to:
  find out what their view is
  discuss if they see there is a problem
  demonstrate the effect their behaviour is having on the other person;
- setting standards for behaviour and monitoring;
- keeping records and using the disciplinary procedure if this soft approach fails.

For someone who is experiencing bullying, if there is no prospect of getting it taken seriously, the last resort is to leave and claim constructive dismissal. Any individual taking this course of action must have kept a log of the reasons for resignation. They will have to prove to a tribunal that they felt they had no option but to leave and had exhausted internal mechanisms of complaint.

## Recipients of bullying

If you are a recipient of bullying, you should:

- get proof and keep a record of all incidents, correspondence and memos;
- establish who you can trust to deal with the problem;
- complain to a manager more senior than the bully;
- share experiences with colleagues and talk to the union;
- dispute the bully's charges or actions in writing;
- show how you think bullying may have affected you in your work.

# Grievance procedures

It is good practice for any organisation to have a formal grievance procedure for staff to use when they feel they have exhausted other mechanisms for sorting out a conflict. Using a formal grievance procedure is not a light thing to undertake, and is rare in my experience. Staff may complain about colleagues' behaviour in many ways, directly and indirectly, but are usually very wary about putting it in writing. Partly they do not feel that the senior managers or Trustees will be able to give a fair or unbiassed resolution to the issue. However, it can be a useful tool in sorting out difficult disputes. (See *Scenarios 1.4, 4.2.*)

The grievance procedure exists to ensure that any work-related problem or grievance can be resolved quickly and fairly.

General points:

- The employee should be able to have a colleague or union representative with them at formal meetings.
- The grievance panel Chair must keep a written record of each meeting. This should include details of the employee's case, the employer's response and the outcome of the meeting.
- At the end of each stage of the grievance procedure, the employee must be advised of the next stage of the procedure by the manager.
- In all stages the time limits may be altered by mutual consent.
- Every effort shall be made to resolve the grievance at each stage, and the proceedings shall be kept confidential to the worker, their representative, the manager and the grievance panel members.
- Copies of correspondence and written records relating to a grievance should be kept for a specified length of time and then destroyed.

# Disciplinary action

Boundaries for personal and professional behaviour need to be established and maintained in all teams. Unfortunately there is no automatic integrity threshold among staff – the organisation and then the line manager have to establish it.

Using formal disciplinary action rather than other more informal methods is going to be appropriate where gross misconduct has taken place, or where there is persistent poor performance, i.e. breaking those personal or professional performance standards and boundaries that have been identified above.

(See *Scenario 1.2.*)

It is not pleasant to tell someone their work or behaviour is not acceptable – but it can be an essential part of management. It is important to practise if you don't feel confident enough to do it. If you need help, ask for it from a more experienced manager. Written disciplinary procedures are necessary to enforce rules of conduct and behaviour at work concerning: standards of behaviour towards other staff; behaving in a non-discriminatory way; and carrying out work in a legal manner and according to set standards and procedures. It follows that employees need to know what these rules and standards are. They should be clearly formulated by the organisation and written down.

- A disciplinary procedure is a management tool. The intention should be to:
  find out what is going wrong and why;

  decide how to put it right;

  get it put right;

  monitor it;

  enable the organisation and employee to get on with the service delivery;

  have the ability to summarily dismiss fairly and quickly following an investigation if gross misconduct is proved.
- The manager should always have a clear analysis of what is going on in each case.
- Procedures should allow for full and unbiassed investigation of any allegation of misconduct or circumstances surrounding a grievance.
- Employees must be allowed to have their trade union representative, or other representative of their choice present at any hearing in which they are involved.
- An appeal process should be built into the procedure after every decision reached.
- Membership of any appeal panel should be different from that of the original disciplinary and grievance panel in order to ensure an unbiassed assessment of the case and any decision reached.
- Employees should be made aware of their legal rights.

## How to conduct a disciplinary interview

Here are some key points that must be followed:

1 The person being judged must have the right to:
hear all evidence against them;
state their case;
have a decision made by a non-biassed person.

2 Tribunals accept that in small organisations it can be difficult to find anyone who is unbiassed, but all effort should be made that the person hearing evidence acts in as unbiassed a way as possible.

3 The interview should be regarded as formal but not a trial.

4 The shape of the interview is as follows:

The employee must be informed of the allegations (they should have had written notice of the allegations already in the letter informing them about the hearing).

The employer may tell the employee what the allegations are, call witnesses or rely on written statements.

The employee should be given the opportunity to question them.

After the employer has set out their information the employee can state their case.

Only in exceptional circumstances such as the employee refusing to attend a hearing would it be fair to give a penalty without hearing the employee's side of the case.

Having heard the case the employer must come to a conclusion about the facts of the case. They can decide that further investigation is necessary at this point.

5 If the employee does not attend the interview but has an excuse acceptable to the employer, the employer should postpone the interview. If the employee does not give a reason, gives an unacceptable reason or persistently misses the interview, the employer may be justified in making a penalty without hearing the employee's case.

6 The employer has to come to a reasonable decision: the case does not have to be proved beyond doubt.

7 The hearing should be adjourned before reaching a decision, to give time for those making the decision to consider the facts.

8 **Factors in reaching a decision** regarding a penalty should include:
full background circumstances relating to the employee, length of service, position, general behaviour;

previous disciplinary hearings, especially those of a similar nature and any warnings which are still outstanding;

how the employer has dealt with similar disciplinary matters in the past – to show consistency;

whether the contract or any other document describes a prescribed penalty for this misconduct;

any relevant reason, excuse, background or circumstance.

9   A **disciplinary warning** is a notice that the employee's work or conduct is unsatisfactory. Whether verbal or written, a warning must always be identified and should include:

the type of conduct or inadequate performance;

the facts found;

whether there is a disciplinary penalty in addition to the hearing;

if appropriate, what changes or improvements are expected;

the time period for the change or improvement and when and how it will be reviewed;

the consequences of further misconduct or lack of improvement;

any right of appeal and the timetable for appeal;

the date after which the warning will be disregarded if work or performance improves and there is no further disciplinary problem or alternatively the fact that it will stay permanently on record.

A **final written warning** must include the statement that the next step, if no improvement occurs will be dismissal. Final written warnings may be kept on file indefinitely.

It is important not to make a blanket specification in the disciplinary procedure about how long records will stay on people's files.

# PART TWO

# Common team conflict scenarios

Not all teams or organisations operate as well as we would like them to. These scenarios are intended to reflect the reality of working and managing in the voluntary sector. They may seem overly complex at times; not all the issues in the conflict are dealt with in one go and not all loose ends are tied up – that is intended to reflect reality.

Each scenario does suggest action, sometimes for one participant sometimes for both. Each scenario follows the same format:

Story
What's going on?
General comments
Issues for managers
What the participants could do next
Useful phrases
Towards a more positive outcome

The scenarios are divided into five sections which are cross-referenced back to the parts of Part 1 that are most relevant to read or re-read.

## Scenario 1  Power imbalances

1.1     Team leader being bullied by her team
1.2     Manager has favourites
1.3     Prejudice
1.4     Team member bullied by their boss

## Scenario 2  Relations with clients

2.1     Violence
2.2     Intervening in a conflict between users

### Scenario 3  Team dynamics

3.1     Team cliques or splits

3.2     Scapegoating

### Scenario 4  Individual differences

4.1     Disagreement on facts and methods

4.2     Differences in values and disrespect

4.3     Personality clash

### Scenario 5  Change management

5.1     A 'stuck' organisation with a new Chair

# The organisations

There are three organisations used in the scenarios. They are figments of my imagination and any resemblance to real organisations or teams is entirely accidental.

**1  CARE4U:** Large care provider with 60 staff in four levels of hierarchy.

| | |
|---|---|
| Martha | *Chief Executive* |
| Simon | *Assistant Director* |
| Frank | *Assistant Director, Finance* |
| Ade | *Line manager* |
| Ian | *Ade's team member* |
| Oona | *Member of the advocacy team* |
| Thomas | *Finance and admin assistant* |
| Judy | *Finance and admin assistant* |

Appears in Scenarios:

1.2  Manager has favourites

1.3  Prejudice

2.1  Violence

5.1  Change management

**2 SAFETYNET:** Small local advice centre. One manager, one deputy, six advisors and two finance and admin staff.

Brian        *Director*
Sam          *Deputy Director*
Josie        *Finance worker*
Hazel        *Finance assistant and receptionist*
Sunil        *Advisor*
Avril        *Advisor*
Tina         *Advisor*
Migwe        *Advisor*

Appears in Scenarios:

1.4 Team member bullied by boss
3.1 Team cliques or splits
4.1 Disagreement on facts and methods
4.3 Personality clash

**3 RANCH HOSTEL:** For young homeless people, with a supported residential unit. Director, four team leaders, 24 staff in four teams, outreach staff.

Ben          *Hostel team leader*
Maia         *Hostel team member*
Yusuf        *Hostel team leader*
Susan        *Outreach team leader*
Steven       *Outreach team member*
Grace        *Women's hostel manager*
Farrida      *Hostel worker*
Anup         *Treasurer*

Appears in Scenarios:

1.1 Team leader being bullied by her team
2.2 Intervening in a conflict between users
3.2 Scapegoating
4.2 Differences in values and disrespect

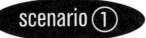

# POWER IMBALANCES

## 1.1 Team leader being bullied by her team

Susan has just been appointed as Ranch Hostel outreach team leader and is having a difficult time beginning to manage her team. Susan is not very experienced in management. She acted as deputy manager of a drop-in centre for drug users for one year prior to getting this job. She previously worked in a local authority setting. She has a radically different approach to outreach and team work from her staff. The previous manager at Ranch Hostel had adopted a very *laissez-faire* management culture and let the team handle the outreach work in ways the staff liked rather than in ways Susan now wants to introduce. There is also an underlying dynamic of different cultures at work. Susan is an older white woman used to local authority management hierarchies and very clear lines of authority. She has risen through the ranks from a secretarial role after returning to work after having children. She does not have a degree, but she has ten years experience in hostel and community work.

Some of her team have been at Ranch since it opened and have known all the staff and Committee since they started. One in particular, Steven, has a very close relationship with the current treasurer of the Committee, Anup. Steven also applied for the post of manager of the outreach team, but did not get it. Susan was not told this before she started managing the team.

Susan has come into post, 'all guns blazing', trying to cover up her nervousness about managing such a team. She introduces a new shift pattern, new reporting mechanisms, new guidelines on contact with residents outside working hours and a new approach to writing up the day book – all in one go without consulting the staff. She says this is because, in her first two weeks in post, she has observed their sloppy style and thinks that boundaries are being infringed with residents. She has the sanction of the Director to 'shake them up', but he probably didn't envisage quite such a draconian approach.

The team meeting is stunned into silence, but Steven looks thunderous and asks her on whose authority these measures are being introduced. When she says 'on my authority', Steven practically walks out of the meeting. He shows through his body language his contempt for her, and generally behaves in an undisciplined way – snorting at her suggestions and undermining her in the team meeting.

After the meeting, Steven decides that Susan's approach is not on and complains to the Treasurer when they meet in the pub that night. Anup then makes enquiries about Susan's management style.

In the next team meeting Susan makes a comment about a person with cerebral palsy that the team is working with 'being crippled by his condition'. Steven immediately leaps in with 'That's not the correct way to look at it – he's crippled by your attitude not by his condition'. Susan responds by saying 'Well that's just your view'. Inside she is embarrassed to have said something thoughtlessly, but has no idea how to show this to her team. She comes over as cold and uncaring. From then on, the team begins to either ignore her or to criticise her increasingly to her face.

Susan's way of responding to their silent insolence or open contempt is to become defensive. Over the next few weeks Susan's life is made a misery by her staff. Steven is 'not quite organising' the staff into a campaign of blocking Susan's decisions, overturning her authority and starting a whispering campaign about her competence. Susan tries talking to the Director but he is not very supportive. He has 'heard' about the original incident but doesn't say from whom and wonders whether she has made an error of judgement in the way she has handled the team. He appears to be dismayed that she couldn't cope with the team and Susan is asked if she really feels she is up to the challenge of working with them.

## What's going on?

| | | |
|---|---|---|
| Nature of difference | ▶ | Ideas about ways of working between team and their leader |
| Reasons for difference | ▶ | Power imbalance |
| | | Inexperienced manager |
| | | Aggrieved team member |
| Any other factors | ▶ | Team clique being openly hostile |
| | | Bullying behaviour by the team |
| | | Undermining of line manager's authority |
| | | Poor induction |
| | | Lack of support for the new manager |
| | | Management culture supports indirect routes of communication |
| | | New manager coming in |
| | | Poor management of change |

# General comments

There are three main issues in this case: a new manager coming into a team who is used to a very different management culture, the manager's lack of expertise in introducing changes to the team, and bullying.

As mentioned in Chapter 5, a recent survey by the University of Stafford found that 78% of people thought they had witnessed bullying at work and half had experienced it. The recent TUC 'bullying at work' hotline has had thousands of calls with complaints ranging from being made to wear a dunce's cap to persistent verbal ridicule. Bullying or ganging up on a team leader is not a common form of bullying, but it can happen: where line management structures are weak, where staff are resentful generally of management, where the team leader is new in post or inexperienced, where the new manager is trying to impose quite radical changes all at once on a team which is very resistant.

Bullying is defined as:

> 'The persistent demeaning and downgrading of human beings through vicious words, and cruel, unseen acts which gradually undermines their confidence and self-esteem.'

(From *Bullying at work*, see *Further Reading*.)

Many grievances may seem trivial, but added together they become a psychological catalogue of horrors. Some of the ways it happens at work are detailed in Scenario 1.4 which considers bullying of a staff member by her boss, i.e. reinforcing the team power position with the extra layer of bullying.

People bully for many reasons. They may feel insecure or stressed, or they may just never have learned a better way. In this case, Steven is bullying because he thinks he knows best, he doesn't like Susan's style, and he seems to be enjoying getting a rise out of Susan, proving her wrong and circumventing the official hierarchy. He also has the support of the team, i.e. weight of numbers.

# Issues for managers

Managers develop a particular style of management which they may recognise or not. This comes about through learning from role models or from the training they may have received in previous organisations. When they come across people who have been managed with a very different style – here they are not used to boundaries or authority – it can be a shock for the team. In this case the team is not ready or willing to change; they feel these changes in style are imposed unreasonably and not in a way that they can accept. The manager, Susan, has failed to recognise the very deep chasm of difference that her style represents to them. What she sees as normal and reasonable, they receive as intrusive and demeaning. Added to the leadership role that Steven is willing to take in opposition to her, this makes for a very challenging set of circumstances for any manager new in post. However there are some strategies she can try. Any manager in this position needs to:

- revise their ideas about introducing such radical changes (for this team) all in one go;
- record their actions carefully so that, if challenged, they can't be denied;
- strengthen their allies;
- ensure the Director knows how bad the situation is as soon as possible;
- document incidents to demonstrate their seriousness;
- make sure that they act openly;
- get support from other senior staff as soon as possible.

If this is not possible, then the manager should work gradually to make boundaries explicit. If the manager introduces a new regulation, for example, regarding making personal calls in work time, then make sure it is applied fairly to all staff members.

For a senior manager observing a line manager getting bullied by their team, it is very important that they use their authority firstly to get the manager's status recognised by the team and secondly to work with the manager to build up their skills in managing. Do not leave them alone to sink or swim. This demonstrates the importance of having regular meetings with line managers to ensure all is working well in the management team.

## What the participants could do next

### Susan

She is now rocked in her self-confidence and frightened to ask for help for fear of being seen to be weak or wrong. When she found out the situation about Steven, she should have gone straight to the Director, documented how serious the situation was and asked for advice or help in sorting out the problem. The longer she did not feel able to do this, the more she lost the nerve to act and worried about seeming foolish and inexperienced. As Steven and the team observe her struggling to manage on her own and not using the allies she might develop, this gives them more power to undermine her self-esteem and her authority. Now that she is being blamed by the Director for the whole problem, she needs to take stock and think through how to act from here. She can:

- keep a diary of incidents;
- tell staff to put complaints in writing;
- monitor their activities normally and not let difficulties pass;
- talk to staff on their own about the issue;
- keep meetings to a minimum and try to anticipate trouble;

- get as many allies as possible;
- use one of the senior staff to help bolster authority;
- contact her union representative;
- if all else fails, make a formal complaint.

## Useful phrases

With the staff in this team acting contemptuously, one of the best tactics is to try and make the issues of snide comments and body language as explicit as possible. Be direct, but not insulting; so say:

'What is your point, can you explain it please?'

'Is there something else you'd like to say because you don't look as though you are comfortable with my point?'

'What do you disagree with specifically?'

'Please put comments to me about the new policy in writing.'

## Towards a more positive outcome

### Team members

- Resist the temptation to collude in team bullying.
- If you are a witness be helpful and give evidence.
- Don't talk about staff behind their back – it's undermining. Talk to them directly about the issue.
- Own your own feelings and opinions in meetings.
- If you don't listen to 'gossip', this diminishes the power of informal networks and patterns of communication.

### Senior managers

- Help less experienced managers rather than throwing them in at the deep end or undermining them.
- Carry out thorough induction programmes for managers as well as staff.
- Resist any tendency by staff to use informal or unorthodox routes of communication to the Trustees or to more senior managers, by-passing the formal line management structures.
- Look at the organisational culture that has allowed this to happen.

### Managers being bullied

Where no one either on the staff or on the Committee seems to be taking it seriously:

- Contact your own trade union.
- Contact the local Council for Voluntary Service.
- Public Concern (see *Resources*) might help if whistleblowing is an issue.
- Make an appointment with a local CAB to sort out your rights if the situation becomes so bad you feel you might have to resign.

# 1.2 Manager has favourites

Frank manages two finance officers and two finance admin support staff, Thomas and Judy. One of the finance officers has announced she is leaving and has handed in her notice. Thomas and Judy are both interested in the opportunity thus created. Thomas has been with Care4U for ten years and has recently moved from being a general admin assistant to his current post. He is reliable if unexciting in his work, and tends to keep much to himself. He is going to night school to get an accountancy qualification, and is doing well in this. Judy has been in post for four years and is hard-working. She doesn't have the same opportunities as Thomas to get trained and has recently begun an affair with Frank. So far this has been kept secret from the office.

Frank offers Judy the post of finance officer at their next supervision session as a promotion. He does not consult anyone about internal appointments policy and regards the decision as within his gift alone. Frank and Judy go out to celebrate and are seen in a compromising position in a night club by one of their colleagues. By Monday morning the rumour is all round the office and the appointment has been announced.

When Thomas hears this he becomes enraged. He can't believe what has happened and that he didn't even get an opportunity to go for the job. His normal quiet demeanour is lost. He storms into Frank's office where Frank is preparing for a senior managers' meeting later that morning. Thomas leans over Frank's desk and says, 'I don't believe what you have done – don't you realise there's a staff policy about internal appointments. And I'm better qualified! And you've given it to your floozy!'

Frank is a bit taken aback and put on the defensive as he didn't realise that the affair had been rumbled. However he also feels both threatened and affronted that this junior staff member can feel able to come into his room and upbraid him in this manner. He replies, 'That's my decision and my choice, and if you don't like it you know what you can do ...'

Thomas responds with, 'Are you threatening me? Don't you realise that I know my rights? I could do you for sexism and corrupt behaviour – and as a Finance Director I think you should be worried about that.'

Frank is now thoroughly irritated and guilty and increasingly angry that Thomas is undermining his power base and questioning his decisions. He shouts, 'If you're so knowledgeable about your rights you can go and read up on them at home – you're suspended for insubordination!'

Thomas walks out in high dudgeon to talk to his union rep, Frank has to have a difficult meeting with the Chief Executive, who is off to a very important fundraising event and doesn't want to be distracted, and the rest of the staff chew over the latest scandal with great glee.

## What's going on?

| | | |
|---|---|---|
| Nature of difference | ▶ | Knowledge of policies |
| | | Views on appropriate management practices |
| | | Different values |
| | | Management culture |
| | | |
| Reasons for difference | ▶ | Power imbalance |
| | | Arrogant manager |
| | | Aggrieved team member with something to prove |
| | | |
| Any other factors | ▶ | Different management style |
| | | Affairs at work with direct line managed staff |
| | | Lack of transparency about decisions on promotion |

## General comments

One of the main contributory factors here is lack of common management culture across the organisation. Frank is a new manager, very able in his own area of expertise, but bringing with him a management culture completely alien to the finance section and to the organisation. His line manager, the Chief Executive, operates a 'hands-off' style of management with her seniors and spends a lot of her time on external rather than internal issues. She has not instituted any regular or formal supervision sessions with him. This means that she has no in-depth knowledge of his management style. She has also not taken time as part of the induction to make explicit the management style and culture that she wants to operate in Care4U. Her lack of knowledge of the resignation and consequent recruitment opportunity in his team and Frank's own eagerness to run things his way have combined to allow this problem to be worse than it might have been.

The additional factor of Frank's affair within his own department adds to the rich mix. Affairs at work, especially with juniors in the same department, or even a close friendship at work where jobs or promotion are in the gift of one partner are clearly a huge risk to maintaining appropriate line relationships with proper boundaries. Confidentiality may be at risk, and the participants are left wide open to accusations of impropriety at least, and corruption at worst.

## Issues for managers

Supervision is always vital even for senior staff, and especially for staff who have entered the organisation from a different sector with a different management culture and expectations. The Chief Executive made her first mistake in not instituting regular supervision sessions for Frank and in not being assertive about the management culture and expectations across the organisation. If an organisation has well developed policies on equal opportunities, recruitment or internal appointments, then these must be well known to managers and used by them effectively. Otherwise this leads to resentments and potentially difficult situations like this one.

Personal relationships at work are a difficult area. If these are between staff who have a close working relationship or who are line managed by one another, this immediately adds a significant layer of potentially inappropriate actions. Even if the pair are scrupulous in their work relationship it leaves them open to accusations of favouritism by other staff.

The combination of Frank's autocratic management style, lack of boundaries on inappropriate personal relationships, lack of understanding of the organisation's policies, short temper and defensive style have got him into very deep water here.

## What the participants could do next

### Thomas

He has gone to see his union representative and has a very good case for complaining of inappropriate suspension and that Frank has broken the organisation's rules and policies on internal appointments. His best route to action is the immediate formal complaints procedure.

### Frank

He is not going to get much support from the Chief Executive and his best defence is that he didn't know that he wasn't allowed to take this action. However his actions towards his subordinate look extremely suspicious. He could face very serious disciplinary charges and possible dismissal.

### Martha

The Chief Executive, has to take a formal route immediately. This gives several signals:

- She knows the organisation's policies and takes them seriously.
- She recognises that this manager has stepped too far out of line to even consider an informal sorting out of the issues.
- Frank's own autocratic action has to be countered strongly – it is not appropriate to react so strongly to an aggrieved employee.
- This should allow the rest of the staff to feel that boundaries which have been crossed are going to be pulled back in line again and help them feel secure.

Martha suspends Frank pending further investigation. She rescinds the suspension of Thomas on the grounds that Frank had no authority to suspend him until he had discussed the issue with her and had it ratified. She carries out an investigation into Thomas's suspension first and finds that there is not enough reason to suspend Thomas. Thomas is brought back to work and a locum Assistant Director, Finance is found to enable the organisation to get ready for audit and recruit a new finance officer following proper internal procedures.

## Useful phrases

In this case, most of the communication will be written by formal memos and letters outlining complaints and giving evidence. Most letters will need to be very carefully worded and the outline of the disciplinary process and formal investigation explained to Frank and Thomas. Where there are meetings face to face they should be before witnesses and carefully documented to head off further mis-communication problems. It will be important to carefully investigate all aspects of this complex case to lessen the likelihood of appeals later. This will need to involve members of staff or Committee members who have not previously been aware of the issues or involved closely with the personalities directly affected.

## Towards a more positive outcome

In some disputes or conflicts, even when they appear to be between two individuals, it is appropriate to move straight to the disciplinary procedure. In this case the situation might have been prevented by:

- regular and formal supervision of senior staff;
- regular senior managers' meetings that discussed management issues formally in order to create a consistent management culture across the organisation;
- formal induction for senior staff into the organisation's policies;
- clear messages about what appropriate boundaries are and expectations on these right from the start.

# 1.3 Prejudice

Ade has been in post at Care4U for six months as a member of the management team. He is the first man of West African origin that has been appointed to a managerial post in the organisation. There are three white men and one white woman at his level. Ade has had many years of experience as a manager in both the private sector and the voluntary sector. He has been working for the past twenty years, for the last ten of those as a manager. He transferred his skills into the voluntary sector out of commitment to the provision of care in his local borough. He has seen nothing but good work by Care4U from the outside. Ade has made a good start as a manager. He has got to know his team and they are now working well together; he has ideas for ensuring that they stick to quality controls better in future and has made a recent presentation to the rest of the senior managers about this project. He feels that he is doing a good job.

However, in spite of his good track record, Ade is beginning to suspect that he is not being managed in the same way as his colleagues. The Assistant Director, Simon, manages him and two of the other line managers. Ade has been asked for detailed timesheets and has his expenses forms checked with a fine toothcomb in each supervision session. He has also had his budgets for his section sent back three times for detailed checking.

As Ade knows that he is the best qualified and most experienced in financial skills among his colleagues, he is getting more suspicious of his manager's behaviour. He asks his fellow line managers, who say that this has never happened to them, not even when they were new in post. Ade now thinks that Simon has a prejudiced attitude towards him and is anxious to deal with it before any more serious consequences occur. He checks with the other managers who have been in Care4U longer and finds that there has been no systematic equal opportunities, anti-racism or managing diversity training in Care4U.

As a new development some of the staff in his team are starting to act as though they don't trust him and are treating his instructions with contempt. He goes to Simon to discuss this, and finds that, firstly, his side of the story is not believed; secondly, the Assistant Director already appears to know all about the staff change of attitude before Ade came to him. Ade later finds out that his team member, Ian, plays squash with Simon each week.

## What's going on?

When staff who are from a minority ethnic group face different treatment from other colleagues, one of the first reasons that springs to mind is prejudice. In this case it could be that the Assistant Director has a stereotyped attitude such as 'West Africans are corrupt' which is why he is closely inspecting anything to do with accounting for money or time. Now it appears that the Assistant Director's attitude has filtered through to Ade's team and is threatening his ability to exercise authority over them as his instructions are gainsaid by his immediate superior.

Nature of difference:     ▶  Differential and prejudiced treatment by line
                              manager
                              Line manager undermining Ade's authority

Reasons for difference:   ▶  Stereotyping
                              Mis-use of power position by a line manager

Any other factors:        ▶  Lack of equal opportunities awareness
                              No anti-racism training for managers
                              No organisational commitment to tackling diversity
                              issues

## General comments

Conflicts of this nature are not uncommon in the sector. They can be very unpleasant and painful, and to ignore the situation or deal with it badly can have severe consequences such as:

- individual stress
- team misfunction and loss of effectiveness
- reduction of trust between individuals from different racial groups in the workplace
- race or sex discrimination cases.

British society is still oppressive and racism is still pervasive in all types of organisations and institutions.

- Not all Boards of Trustees appreciate the need to tackle racism within the organisation as well as in their service delivery.
- Not all managers are aware of the issues or have a sophisticated analysis of the nature of oppression or how their acts may be oppressive.
- Not everyone knows how to be aware and act as an anti-racist.
- Not everyone wants to be aware.

The background to diversity issues in the workplace is not neutral. We live in a society that broadly facilitates being white and being male and being straight, and does not facilitate being any other way to the same extent. Individuals may make themselves exceptions to this but may still face discrimination and prejudice simply on the grounds of their gender or race or some other personal characteristic in spite of their personal achievements.

There will be conflicts at work where issues of diversity are either a central concern or operate as an undertow to the conflict. For example:

'You do not listen to my ideas because I am a woman.'

'I find the fact that you check my work more often than that of my colleagues at best an irritation and at worst an insult. I suspect that this may be because I am black and they are white like you.'

## Issues for managers

Dealing with conflict effectively is a difficult management task at any time, but dealing with this sort of conflict is particularly fraught. There are many opportunities for mis-communication, and managers may be reluctant to intervene because they fear:

- it might make it worse;
- their own prejudices might be brought into play;
- they will be called biassed;
- they lack awareness;
- they lack skills.

Whilst individual managers' fears should not excuse them from the responsibility of acting appropriately, they may need to be taken into account in a conflict like this. Cases where there is direct or indirect discrimination, harassment or victimisation have to be handled directly by the internal disciplinary process or by law. However, there are situations where formal or legal redress may not be the first step to take. People who are on the receiving end of discrimination may sometimes prefer some form of mediation as a first step in a dispute, for example: where the issue involves diversity and:

- misinterpretation
- culture or language issues
- people feeling 'rubbed up' the wrong way
- style differences.

However the basic building blocks favouring mediation would have to be in place. (See *Chapter 5, Toolkit for managers.*)

This particular scenario is already escalating beyond the senior manager treating Ade differently in supervision to his actively undermining Ade's management of his team. This could very quickly lead to a potential case for indirect discrimination as the Assistant Director starts to treat Ade in ways which may affect his annual appraisal, chance of promotion or pay, or even if Ade's reputation in the organisation is affected by any snide comments by his superior.

Any senior manager has to take all allegations of prejudice, discriminatory behaviour or oppression seriously. The other most positive step is a long-term programme of staff training which is focused on changing behaviour. If this message is played out loud and clear in the organisation, then prejudiced managers or staff will have a harder time exercising their attitudes. If a strong lead is not given it can result in situations like this happening.

## What the participants could do next

### Ade

The first dilemma for Ade is whether or not to go to his own manager or indeed straight to a senior manager. The downside of this course of action is:

- He might not get any support.
- Possible responses from his manager are mainly negative.
- The organisation has no strong tradition of recognising and dealing with diversity issues.

Other tactics he might use to make the potential outcomes more positive, instead of just reflecting back on him as an individual, are:

- Making it an issue beyond one person's management - i.e. looking at other diversity issues – not to ignore his own treatment but to widen the argument.
- Getting the personnel department involved.
- Getting the support of his colleagues.
- Documenting the way he is treated and going to internal grievance procedure.

Ade decides both to get the support of his colleagues and to tackle the issue up-front in the next supervision. He prepares carefully for the meeting and for a set of outcomes he will accept. If the manager denies the different treatment or his intervention in his team and refuses to change his style, then as a next step, Ade will go to the personnel department or senior manager with a formal complaint.

## Useful phrases

Some ideas for the types of wording Ade could use:

> 'Is there an issue about how I fill in my timesheets, because you seem to pay a lot of attention to them at every supervision meeting? Jane happened to mention that she doesn't have hers checked in this way.'
> 'Are you checking up on me?'
> 'I was just wondering if there is any reason for mine being checked and Jane's not being checked.'

(This is pinning the person down. If they say 'yes', they are scuppering themselves. If they say 'no', then Ade can go on to say how he would like it to happen in the future.)

> 'I feel you are undermining my authority by discussing line management issues directly with my staff – I would like this sorted out.'

These are possible opening statements for Ade, who is operating in a hostile environment. In this scenario, Ade takes a tactical stand in beginning by not mentioning the issue of stereotyping. If the manager goes on to be unable to justify his actions or makes a directly prejudiced remark, then Ade has decided to go on to challenge him directly on stereotyping.

Obviously the other route is to go straight to a senior manager or personnel manager and discuss the issue with them. Ade then does not have to face his manager alone or without getting a better idea of how the senior levels of the organisation are reacting to Simon's prejudiced management.

However, there may be times when prejudice is such that nothing short of the grievance procedure or harassment procedure and/or union support will do. In this case, getting support and back-up for the person who is making the allegations is important, either through the union or through staff groups. In a collusively racist environment, management are more likely to take prejudice seriously where they can see that it is not one black person's word against a white person's.

## Towards a more positive outcome

Getting behind stereotypes has to be a continuous process. 'We can only hint at the kind of emotional and psychological changes which are necessary to replace long-standing, ingrained stereotypes and prejudices with more accurate, fair and complete views of people.' (*Constructive Conflict Management*, see *Further Reading.*)

Dealing with conflicts of this nature is part of a diversity strategy in that it is part of a process of prejudice reduction and increasing awareness of how communication methods affect people. It encourages attitudes such as 'My way is not the right way; it is just one way.' It benefits individuals through giving them an insight into their own attitudes and prejudices. It benefits organisations in terms of recognition of a major cause of stress and workforce turnover.

In cases like this one, take the following steps:

- Make sure managing diversity is on the agenda at work.
- Treat all cases seriously and investigate.
- Offer some form of mediation or dispute resolution first if the person making the allegation would welcome a more informal approach to begin with.
- Set ground-rules about process and outcomes and confidentiality.
- Always move to the disciplinary procedure if mediation is not appropriate or if the outcomes of mediation are not satisfactory.
- Have a clear set of guidelines about which technique is appropriate when.
- If you are a colleague, be supportive of colleagues who are facing prejudice.

# 1.4 Team member bullied by their boss

SafetyNet is a small local advice centre, which has been going for fifteen years. It was set up as a local community resource in the mid 1980s. They have a stable staff who are very committed to the local community. They are based in a Neighbourhood Centre on a large estate on the edge of town and are relatively isolated from the rest of the City's voluntary sector.

Finance worker Josie is in the kitchen shouting at Hazel, the Finance assistant and receptionist. 'Why didn't you remember to set the computer back-up running last night? There was a power cut this morning and all the invoices I did yesterday are lost! Now I'll have to do that work all over again. Why won't you learn! You stupid girl.' Josie stomps off to the computer to re-do the work and Hazel runs down to the toilets to cry. She returns to find that the phones are ringing and no one is covering them. 'Hazel, get the phone! Where have you been?'

Hazel thinks, 'Another cheery day in the office! Why does she always have to be getting at me!' Later in the week, Josie delegates to Hazel a report for the management committee on the number and type of callers to the advice centre. Hazel has never done such a report before, but is scared to go back and ask Josie how to do it because she fears Josie's reaction again. She hands in the report on the day the papers are due to be sent out. Josie comes back at 4.00pm and says she hasn't done it in the right format. She should have used the spreadsheet programme to do pie charts. Why didn't she look back at the last report? And then she tears up Hazel's work in front of her and says she'll now have to do it herself and Hazel will have to stay late to help send out the committee papers. As Hazel and Josie work together in an office, none of the other staff really know how bad things are getting. In any case the team is split over the Legal Aid Contract issue and barely talking to each other at the best of times. (See *Scenario 3.1*.)

Hazel is getting more and more unhappy in her work and in her job. Josie is never as nasty to anyone else in the organisation. Although she can be sharp with the others and 'tick them off' it is never as bad as it is with Hazel. Hazel wants to leave, but the money at the centre is actually a bit better than she would get in most other typing and receptionist jobs and she and her partner have just taken on a big mortgage.

One day the Centre Manager walks in in the middle of a major 'dressing down' that Josie is giving to Hazel and is shocked enough to ask to see Hazel on her own later that day. Josie hisses at her afterwards that she'd better not make a complaint or things will only get worse. Hazel is in two minds whether to say anything or not, but in the end she can't help herself. Brian, the Director, is so skilled at asking her questions that she bursts into tears and tells him the full story.

## What's going on

Nature of difference  ▶  Nitpicking and bullying manager

Reasons for difference  ▶  Power imbalance

Any other factors  ▶  General undermining of staff
No close senior management checking what's going on

## General comments

Bullying is defined as:

'The persistent demeaning and downgrading of human beings through vicious words, and cruel, unseen acts which gradually undermines their confidence and self-esteem.'

(From *Bullying at work*, see *Further Reading*.)

Bullying can seem trivial to people who are not on the receiving end of it. Often small incidents added together seem much worse. This issue is also discussed in Chapter 5, *Toolkit for Managers, Bullying*.

These are some of the ways bullying happens at work.

**Managerial:** Unconstructive criticism, undermining in front of colleagues, undermining authority.

**Emotional:** Excluding, ridicule or humiliation.

**Verbal:** Inappropriate language or tone of voice.

People act in a bullying way for many reasons. They may not feel they can get results in any other way; they may feel insecure or stressed; or they may just never have learned a better way.

The consequences of bullying can be bad for the organisation, bringing:

■ high staff turnover
■ less concern with quality
■ low morale
■ lack of creative input
■ loss of initiative.

At the personal level, persistent bullying can result in:

■ depression
■ low self-esteem
■ shyness
■ poor work achievement

- isolation
- sleeplessness
- other stress related symptoms such as difficulty in concentrating, repetitive minor illnesses
- absenteeism
- and at worst – threatened or attempted suicide.

Unchecked bullying also damages the bully, who learns that they can get away with violence, aggression and threats and that this sort of behaviour gets them what they want.

Bullying has been likened to a form of brainwashing where victims end up believing that somehow they deserve to be bullied. People on the receiving end can feel vulnerable and powerless. Their self-esteem may have been considerably damaged especially if the bullying has been going on for some time.

## Issues for managers

Take notice of the signs of bullying including:

- a recent change in atmosphere
- a change in employees' attitude
- increased absenteeism
- increased staff turnover
- less concern with quality and productivity
- a change in level of staff complaints.

Action to take can include:

- making it clear to employees that managers recognise bullying can be a problem;
- identifying what is reasonable behaviour and establishing disciplinary procedures for unreasonable actions;
- believing staff when they complain of bullying and supporting them through the investigation and disciplinary process;
- reassuring the bullied that they can't be further intimidated;
- providing counselling for the victim to help them recover and regain lost confidence and for the bully to help them recognise and alter their behaviour;
- ensuring that job descriptions are secure and unequivocal.

(See also *Chapter 5, Toolkit for Managers, Bullying.*)

## What the participants could do next

### Hazel

She told the Director what was going on, but was reluctant to make a formal complaint against Josie. She still has to work there. She now has to trust that Brian will make it clear to Josie that her management style has been unacceptable. Josie may not change or may slip into her old ways again after a few days or weeks. She may even act vindictively towards Hazel. Hazel can:

- establish who she can trust to deal with the problem;
- keep a record of all incidents;
- complain to a more senior manager or Committee member and if it resurges again;
- share experiences with colleagues;
- talk to her union rep;
- send Josie a memo disputing charges or actions;
- keep copies of all correspondence;
- show how bullying has affected her work.

## Useful phrases

If you are being bullied and feel that you could try to tackle some of the issues on your own, try using some of the techniques below. Generally it is always a good idea to document incidents and get help as soon as possible from the union or a senior manager or Committee member that you can trust.

Say you don't like it and it is not appropriate:

'Don't treat me like this.'
'Shouting at me is not appropriate.'
'I'll listen to you if you speak to me with respect.'
'Don't shout.'

Ask direct questions pointing out what is going on:

'Why are you so angry?'
'What do you expect to happen?'
'Why are you humiliating me?'

Say what you feel:

'I feel intimidated.'
'I feel you treat me differently.'
'I feel de-skilled by your behaviour.'

Point out your view of what has gone wrong:

'You asked me to act beyond my level of responsibility.'
'The deadline was too tight.'

'You didn't give me the right instructions.'

Say how you would like it done better in future:

'I can't work productively if I'm shouted at; please don't do it.'
'Please delegate with more time for deadlines.'
'Please show me how you want it laid out.'

Finally, point out that if it carries on you will make a formal complaint.

## Towards a more positive outcome

The power of the bully is often to silence others through fear. Even where there is a grievance procedure staff may be too frightened to use it, so organisations must adopt a clear strategy. Senior managers must ensure that policies or codes of conduct refer explicitly to bullying. Staff should treat each other with dignity and respect, and behaviour which is demeaning, demoralising, intimidating or unfair should be treated as harassment. Some organisations have set up a network of staff to support victims of bullying, offering a listening and advisory service. This confidential, informal support may help the victim to identify what is happening as bullying, and may encourage them to use formal channels if appropriate.

A complaint should always be taken seriously. Many employees feel they will not be believed, and will hesitate to bring up issues or complaints which may on their own seem trivial. For the bullied, using the formal grievance procedure may be the only way to stop persistent bullying.

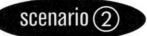
# RELATIONS WITH CLIENTS

## 2.1 Violence

Oona is an advocacy worker at Care4U. She works from a local office and is part of the county-wide advocacy team. The team supports people needing care in their own homes in getting access to benefits and support that they would not otherwise have. She is going on a visit to a Mr and Mrs Jones whom she has not visited before. Care4U has not been running the advocacy service for long and Oona has not done this type of work before. They do not have a special set of guidelines on health and safety at work or on visiting new clients, nor on someone knowing where staff are at all times, nor has Oona had any special training. However she has worked in the care professions a long time, has experience of dealing with 'difficult' clients and has not had any situations she couldn't handle in the past.

She arrives at the Jones' at 4pm to find that only Mrs Jones is in. She seems very friendly and they get a cup of tea and Oona starts to explain about the services that she can offer the Jones. They need advice about how to get repairs done on their house and on their entitlement to benefits, etc. Mrs Jones is not very mobile and needs extra physiotherapy and a walking frame after her recent hospital stay. Then Mr Jones appears in the room. He is a big man, and seems to be angry about something. He addresses Mrs Jones, 'What the f*** are you doing talking to that do-gooder – we never needed help before – I told you not to do it.'

He lunges towards Mrs Jones and would have hit her if she hadn't dodged. However he seems too drunk to do much harm. Oona gets up and says 'I don't think there's any call for that.' She realises that she is in a corner of the room away from the door, with no other way out, and that no one knows where she is. Her heart is racing and her palms sweating. Mrs Jones seems used to this behaviour and shouts back, 'P*** off Fred, don't be so rude, and go and sleep it off.' Mr Jones reels back, trips himself into the sofa and sits down with a thump. Oona can't decide whether to run and get out as fast as possible or stay and help Mrs Jones. Is he in the 'falling over drunk' stage or really still capable of causing his wife and her damage?' Mr Jones decides he can't get up or can't be bothered to get up, but fixes Oona with a stare and hisses, 'Get out you stupid B*****. Don't you come back here, you scum.'

Oona, after her adrenaline rush, feels too shocked to say or do anything and goes towards the door. Mrs Jones manages to balance herself up on her sticks and follows her out. She apologises for 'the old soak, you take no notice of him, dear', and asks Oona in a relatively normal voice when she'll be back to sort out her benefits. Still unable to frame coherently all the conflicting things she wishes to say about the incident, Oona says she'll write to her, asks if she'll be all right, and heads off to her own car up the road.

Back at the office, no one else is in. All phone lines to other staff are engaged and Oona begins to go over her experience on her own. She doesn't write it up as a formal report, because that is not office policy. She starts to think of how inadequate her own response was, what she should do to protect Mrs Jones, how to get the old man into a treatment programme. By the end of half an hour she has convinced herself that she was mostly at fault in panicking and behaving in a cowardly way.

## What's going on?

Nature of difference ▶ Opinions
Attitudes

Reasons for difference ▶ Values and attitudes towards 'help'

Additional factors ▶ Lack of support for staff
Lack of trained staff
Drunk clients
Lack of professional boundaries and health and
safety policies

## General comments

The client may be abusive, but poor organisational policies are a primary issue here. Violence at work is increasing; a recent TUC survey of safety representatives found that 46% of issues brought to safety reps in the voluntary sector concerned violence at work. It is extremely important to have policies and practices that protect employees who may come into contact with violence or the threat of violence. They must be trained, supported and protected by organisational policy and procedures.

The Health and Safety Executive defines violence at work as 'any incident in which an employee is abused, threatened or assaulted by a member of the public in circumstances arising out of the course of their employment'. The threat of violence and verbal abuse may be just as damaging or stressful as an actual assault. A work culture that is positive about health and safety and deals in an up-front way with the risk of potential violence to its staff is a good one. Some characteristics are:

■ commitment to Health and Safety Risk Assessment and follow up;
■ an open climate for discussion of cases and being able to admit difficulties or doubts about clients;

- a clear policy on dealing with potential violence;
- training for staff and adequate staffing cover;
- adequate and monitored reporting procedures for case workers/outreach staff;
- supervisors skilled in debriefing;
- a culture which does not blame the victim;
- provision of external counselling after critical incidents, if required.

## Issues for managers

Care4U were very quick to take on a tempting pot of money from the local authority for providing an advocacy service for people who are house-bound. Getting the money fits in with their desire to be the leader in their field and the best care agency in the county. However the competence of their fundraising manager outstrips the ability of the resource manager in recruiting for and supporting an advocacy project.

Organisations developing outreach, care services, home-care services, advocacy services, advice services, hostels, residential homes or any service which delivers services to clients in their own homes needs to take risk assessment and dealing with potential violence very seriously indeed. A few staff in these situations in voluntary organisations have been killed, some wounded and some left with immense physical and psychological scars by being exposed to risks that they were not trained to handle. Not all violence can be prevented, but good policies and preparation of staff is vital.

Here are particular risk factors cited in *Office Health and Safety* (see *Further Reading*):

- Working alone.
- Job location: people whose jobs involve visiting clients in their own home or making inspections carry a risk of aggressive and violent behaviour.
- Hours of work: where people are required to work out of hours or unusual hours.
- Type of job: jobs which can involve restricting the freedom of individual members of the public, collecting rent, dealing with rent or benefit arrears, complaints, housing needs, etc. carry an increased risk of violence.
- Waiting and queuing.
- Name badges: where people wear name badges, they may be traced and threatened outside the workplace.
- Lack of privacy.

Under the Health and Safety at Work Act employers have a duty to carry out risk assessments for their employees, including those employees who face a predictable risk of violence. Regulations state that where risks have been found, preventative measures must be designed to control the risk. The employer must also provide training to all employees on health and safety, the risks involved and possible preventative or protective measures. Employers have a legal duty to report officially violent incidents leading to physical injury under the RIDDOR Regulations (1995).

## What the participants could do next

### Oona

She needs to report this incident to her team leader. The team leader needs to take it seriously. It would be very unhealthy for Oona to carry any feelings of blame for herself or possible inadequacies in how she handled the situation. The organisation has acted irresponsibly in taking on advocacy work and in recruiting inexperienced staff and failing to train them or to take seriously its responsibilities for risk assessment. It could exacerbate her risks if she goes back to the Jones' seeing the issue as a personal failure, without getting guidance, help and support from her line manager.

## Useful phrases

As a general rule, when in a difficult situation where you feel threatened, you should aim not to escalate the situation further by spoken words, body language or movement. Try showing that you are listening to the person by making eye contact, and let them run out of steam. Try repeating a phrase over and over again (the 'broken record' technique).

'I am listening'
'I have heard you'
'I can see that you are angry'
'Strong feelings are OK, shouting at Karen isn't'

If the risk of assault is judged to be imminent you should move further away quickly and decisively. Trust your instincts!

## Towards a more positive outcome

Core policy themes in organisations that care about staff facing violence should be:

- A definition of violence – including verbal abuse.
- An expression of organisational responsibility to assess risks to staff and tackle them.
- A clear identification of those responsible for risk assessment.
- A training programme for all staff likely to face violence, those dealing with the public, and those going into people's homes, using realistic case studies of the likely scenarios, and how to recognise warning signs.
- Preventative measures, including clear team protocols on information about where staff are going.
- Clear responsibility for dealing with incidents and availability of counselling, support and legal help if necessary.

# 2.2 Intervening in a conflict between users

Ranch Hostel runs a specialist unit for young women with children who have become homeless. There are places for five women and up to ten children. Sometimes the hostel is crowded and sometimes relatively empty. Women can stay for up to six months before move-on accommodation is found for them.

This turnover of residents means that there are often tensions in the hostel. Usually the group of women who have been there the longest tend to make the arrangements run their way and try and get the first go with the washing machine and the first turn at cooking etc. A hidden 'pecking order' can arise which can make the atmosphere unwelcoming to newcomers. The staff work with the residents on this issue with varying degrees of success. The staff work on a rota basis, except for the manager, Grace, who is on duty every week day, but can't always be on site as she has management meetings and external forums to attend. There are no staff present at the hostel at night, although they can be called out in an emergency via mobile phone.

Farrida, one of the hostel workers, has reported to Grace that two of the women residents are rubbing each other up the wrong way and that this might get out of hand. Sarah has been in the hostel for four weeks and has a little girl, Ruth, aged three, who is very withdrawn and quiet most of the time. Margie is a new resident and has a boy, aged five, called Billy. Billy is very active, often wild and out of control. Margie is very depressed and seems to be unable to relate in a balanced way to Billy – she either ignores him or shouts at him. The staff have already tried to work with her on this but nothing has changed yet.

Grace is working in the office one morning and realises that an angry scene is developing in the lounge between Sarah and Margie. She leaves the office immediately to find Sarah is standing over Margie, shouting at her. Margie has her face in her hands and is crying and cringing. Sarah is shouting, 'Your f***ing kid is out of control, he's always winding her up and now your Billy has hit my Ruth. He'll grow up just like his f***ing dad, won't he. You've got no control over him.' Farrida is in the lounge, and there are several children hovering in the background in the hall.

Farrida seems rooted to the spot unable to say anything. She is attempting to comfort Margie and now Sarah turns on her and shouts, 'You would take her side, wouldn't you ...' She carries on ranting at either Margie or Farrida. Grace shuts the door of the lounge and goes up to Sarah and says directly and firmly, 'Stop shouting'. She carries on saying this in a low but calm voice until Sarah runs out of steam. Then Grace takes her aside and says she'd like to talk to her when she's calmed down and suggests she goes out for a walk or a lie down in her room.

Farrida is still comforting Margie and they are both very shaken. Grace says that she would also like to talk to Margie when she has recovered and to Farrida when the incident is sorted out as far as it can be. Grace then goes out to check on the behaviour of both the children with the children's worker, Toni.

## What's going on?

| Nature of difference | ▶ | Perceptions of how children should behave |
|---|---|---|
| Reasons for difference | ▶ | Values and attitudes towards childcare<br>Blaming child's actions on mother |
| Additional factors | ▶ | Pressure of a hostel environment<br>Pressure of being homeless<br>Depression<br>Lack of personal assertiveness<br>Unconfident staff |

## General comments

Intervention involves taking direct action to put yourself at the heart of a conflict where you see that it is counterproductive to let it continue (see *Chapter 5, Toolkit for Managers, Intervenor*). An intervention process aims to be an empowering experience for both parties rather than a blaming or scapegoating process. Ideally the intervenor will be modelling good practice so that the individuals will be able to solve their own conflicts more creatively and with more positive outcomes in future.

Mediation, however, is a neutral tool (see *Chapter 5, Toolkit for Managers, Mediation*). This is a longer process that aims to provide an opportunity for both parties to explore more about the nature of their differences and to come to a mutually agreed position for future interactions. It requires people to be trained in mediation skills.

Conditions for a mediation process:

- any agreements have to be to the satisfaction of the parties concerned and the parties must agree a resolution is needed;
- the content of the mediation is confidential to the parties (although any agreement may need to be seen by the manager in this type of dispute – but the process might simply be about exploring differences in which case no notes need to be seen);
- the mediator is neutral and impartial and has to be seen as such throughout the proceedings;
- the process is voluntary;
- mediation is 'without prejudice', i.e. the parties can reserve the right to invoke other measures;
- the parties must have the authority to settle.

In this case it was appropriate for Grace to intervene in the immediate highly charged conflict between the residents. Then she may want to mediate between them to sort out more about the root of the problem.

## Issues for managers

When working in a pressured environment with clients or residents who may be under pressure themselves, it is important to learn how to intervene in conflicts that are abusive to one party or that are seeking to blame one party for legitimate differences. Interventions in these cases are never easy and can be highly charged. Safety concerns for staff must also come first. Managers must develop detailed guidelines for staff who may be expected to work in this type of environment to help them to protect themselves and decide on the best course of action in any circumstance.

## What the intervenor could do

The most skilled interventions involve a process of modelling good conflict resolution techniques.

Sample steps in an intervention and mediation process (repeated from *Chapter 5, Toolkit for Managers, Intervenor*).

1   Notice what is going on and say something. This may mean using a repetition technique to gain the attention of the participants who may be shouting at each other. Use a simple form of words, such as 'Calm down'; 'Don't shout'; 'I want you to stop'. And keep repeating until they run out of steam (the 'broken record' technique).
2   Separate the parties to allow a cooling off.
3   Talk to each party separately in neutral terms about what was happening. Do not collude in blaming, name-calling or in any oppression that may be happening at this point.
4   Try and bring each person to an understanding of what is going on between them and what they would like to see as a solution.
5   If both are willing, bring them together to facilitate a reconciliation and a solution that both find acceptable. Use mediation skills to work out what they want to do rather than what you want to impose as long as point 6 is met. (For a sample Mediation Process see *Chapter 5, Neutral Mediator*.)
6   Always keep the parameters within the organisation's rules and procedures.
7   You may need to intervene more than once between people before they can really hear each other's point-of-view.

## Useful phrases

'What is going on?'

'Am I missing something?'

'I can see you're heated, but ...'

'I don't think that it is OK to ...' or 'it is not appropriate to ...'

'I don't understand.'

'Do you mean that ...?'

'I can hear that you're angry, but the way you're dealing with it is damaging X.'

'Shouting is not OK.'

## Towards a more positive outcome

- Always notice what is going on in potentially difficult situations.
- Be proactive and don't prevaricate.
- Don't make assumptions about the other's position or reasons for their position – ask!
- Create space and buy time.
- Be informed and know procedures.
- Acknowledge your emotions and theirs.
- Don't demonise or scapegoat.
- Separate the behaviour from the person.
- Aim to empower others to deal with their own conflict issues.

As the same residents get more skilled in managing conflicts themselves, any interventions should be kept to a minimum – it's better that they learn to do it themselves rather than rely on your intervention.

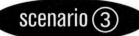

# TEAM DYNAMICS

## 3.1 Team cliques or splits

SafetyNet is a small local advice centre, which has been going for fifteen years. It was set up as a local community resource in the mid 1980s. They have a stable staff who are very committed to the local community. They are based in a Neighbourhood Centre on a large estate on the edge of town and are relatively isolated from the rest of the City's voluntary sector. The local authority advice unit in the city centre thinks that they are not effective and not giving the best type of advice, and in the past has tried to get them to give advice in a different way. The Director, Brian, has been in post for seven years. His preferred management style is consensus. He is good at local politics and preserving the centre, but he recognises that there are threats on the horizon that are serious and looming rapidly.

SafetyNet is facing a big dilemma for its near future. The local authority has decided to completely re-organise the pattern of advice provision. It will now offer contracts for tender covering specific regional areas. One of the regions covers their patch, but if SafetyNet tenders they will have to move to council premises and provide advice on a strict contract basis that pays them per enquiry. At present 75% of their funding comes from the local authority.

If they do tender they would have to expand and be more bureaucratic in their case recording and monitoring of outputs. The Director, Brian, and four of the six advice staff want to pursue the tender development options. The Deputy Director, Sam, and the other advice workers want to stay locally based, are desperately worried about the implications for the relatively non-hierarchical way of working and how they have to relate to their clients. The two finance and admin staff are also split.

At the first few staff meetings to discuss the future options, it was barely possible for the Director to keep hold of the agenda, let alone get agreement on what to present to the Committee. Brian is incredibly busy trying to secure other funding and writing monitoring reports and has asked the Deputy Director to draft a paper on the issues, which Sam doesn't want to do. Sam eventually drafts a paper two weeks after the initial deadline and tables it at the next staff meeting. Brian realises that it is not a balanced paper: it primarily sets out Sam's point of view and puts taking up the tender options in negative terms. Sam has included other possible sources of funds such as a lottery bid and finance from the Health Authority to do anti-poverty work. Brian stays late the night before the crucial staff meeting to write the opposing arguments.

At the staff meeting all workers attend and they sit down two sides of the room as if on opposing sides. The arguments in the two papers are rehearsed and it becomes clear that some of the staff feel that their fundamental values about advice, the centre, and work itself are being threatened. The debate gets very heated and staff become increasingly emotional saying things like: 'I didn't come here to work like this', 'This goes against everything I believe in', 'The Centre's values will be completely compromised', 'I can't be forced to work like a sausage factory', 'I'm not moving into the council centre', 'If we don't tender we'll have to shut – it's the only option'.

Brian sees that he is going to have to do something to defuse this situation. The team is already split with six staff for the tender option and three against. While Brian realises he can overrule his staff, he would prefer them to move forward together rather than impose a solution.

## What's going on?

| | | |
|---|---|---|
| Nature of difference | ▶ | The future of SafetyNet |
| | | Values about ways of working |
| | | Goals for SafetyNet |
| Reasons for difference | ▶ | Different staff values |
| | | Local government funding re-organisation |
| Any other factors | ▶ | Fears about potential bureaucracy |
| | | Fears about change |
| | | Cliques |

## General comments

A threat to an organisation can bring out underlying tensions that were always there, but didn't matter – or in quieter times did not need to be exposed or discussed. Brian is a director whose style emphasises consensus and this is how he has run his organisation up to present. This has worked well in the past and Brian has got out of the habit of setting clear boundaries about who has the final word on decision making. Consensus is difficult to achieve when issues highlight opposing firmly held values. One group will have to compromise.

Brian needs to try to get away from the personal loyalties he has to his decision-making structure and to any members of staff he favours. He should not be seen to be taking sides strongly at the beginning. If he does, this could alienate the staff holding the other point of view. It is important for managers in this situation to get and maintain some form of distance from any decision-making process.

In this case Brian has not emphasised the role of the Committee in making such an important decision. He is used to being in sole charge and his Committee is very locally-based rather than involving outsiders or people with specialist skills. This sort of Committee might have worked for a small local centre, but won't for a bigger, less local advice centre. Generally the role of manager is to be more on the side of the Committee than on that of the staff when there are difficult decisions to be taken.

## Issues for managers

Management boundaries in this case have been let slip into a comfortable but lop-sided role for the current Director. This may work when things are going smoothly, but rapidly shows up flaws when there are crucial and difficult decisions to take. When there is a big decision to be made affecting the whole nature of the organisation the Committee should have been consulted first, and then the staff. The manager has let slip his thinking about the difference between:

informing staff
consulting staff
negotiating with staff
formal organisational decision-making processes.

Being comfortable with what is going on is not the same as making the best decision for the organisation.

## What the participants could do next

### The Committee

They need to re-take control of the final decision-making process without losing entirely the goodwill of the staff who are on opposing sides in the conflict. If they can be seen to want to listen to both perspectives and then to take the decision with clearly documented reasons that safeguard the best outcome for the SafetyNet clients, the staff on the opposing side will most likely come round or at least be able to accept that their voice was heard. If the Committee do not make an effort to hear both sides, they will build up resentments and possible future bitter conflicts. The process of resolving conflict needs to be enabling for the organisation's health as well as the individuals involved.

### The manager

Where there is only one manager operating between the staff group and the Management Committee, this role can become extremely uncomfortable with both sides pulling the manager towards their perspective. The manager may also be used as a conduit for presenting unpopular messages from one side to the other.

This is a dangerous position to be put in. Where boundaries have broken down in a conflict the manager needs to:

- Re-clarify what the nature of decision-making boundaries are with the staff.
- Remember that if the staff group are split, then getting consensus may not be possible.
- Put the issues to the Committee. If there is no clear outcome here, it may be worth while getting a team facilitator in to help with:

  clarifying the best decisions to be made;

  suggesting a clear process for making the decisions and for future decision making.

## Useful phrases

'I am consulting staff on this issue – I welcome your considered feedback, but the final decision must rest with the Committee.'

'It is not possible for all staff to exercise individual control over the value base of the organisation, especially when major changes are in the offing.'

'I welcome all points of view and will put points to the Committee.'

'I prefer a consensus decision-making process, but in this instance where we are so divided, this does not seem possible. As the decision rests with the Committee I will put both points of view to them as staff opinions when presenting them with the options.'

## Towards a more positive outcome

- Where big decisions have to be made – take action sooner rather than later.
- Always make sure a manager sticks to management boundaries even when they seem hopelessly formal – the habit pays off in testing times.
- Ensure the Committee is balanced and able to take decisions, and willing to take responsibility for the consequences for manager and staff of the decisions they do make.
- If the situation seems to be getting out of control – get help from an outside facilitator sooner rather than later, and be very clear about the nature of their involvement.

# 3.2 Scapegoating

In Ranch Hostel there are two hostel teams, one managing a supportive short-stay hostel for women and one an emergency direct-access nightshelter. Maia, one of the women's hostel team, has moved over to the nightshelter team to gain more wide-ranging experience. Maia is the youngest, newest member of the team and one of only two women out of six staff. The client group for the nightshelter are predominantly male, older and may be drunk or generally exhibiting more 'challenging' and up-front behaviour than she has been used to dealing with in the past. Maia has developed a particular style of working with the clients which is more approachable than some of the other staff. She is keen to relate to them, to talk to them and generally acts in a more friendly and accessible way than most of the other staff. The rest of the team think she is 'soft' and making herself open to manipulation and potential threats from the client group. The general attitude is that 'she'll learn the hard way – we won't spend any time helping her out'.

Over the first three months that she is in the team there are several incidents affecting the team's service delivery and 'reputation', all of which happen when Maia is on shift.

- Two members of staff are locked in the office by an angry client.
- There is a tense situation that escalates into a fight.
- Some petty cash money is unaccounted for.

The team begins to attach increasing amounts of blame for these incidents to Maia, not necessarily saying so to her face, but sometimes making snide remarks in her hearing.

'She forgot the safety rule about leaving keys in the office door.'
'She didn't have the bottle to intervene between the residents.'
'She left the petty cash tin out and unlocked.'
'She is soft on the hard luck stories they all come up with.'

The general culture of this team is macho: they like to think they can cope with any challenge; they have a high degree of commitment to the client group; they wear Doc Marten boots and jeans at all times and 'hang out' together in the pub after work more often than not – especially on a Friday night. The team manager has risen from the ranks, is a product of the culture, and fosters this image of the team to itself and within Ranch. The worker before Maia, Pam, left after only six months in post.

Staff now start coming to the team leader, Ben, and saying that they don't want to be on shift with Maia. They say variously that she is unreliable, she is getting the team a bad name, she's like Pam, and she never comes down the pub with them. They forget to mention the odd times that they themselves are in the wrong– and when someone else puts a mistake down to Maia, no one challenges it. Some of them start to tease her about being the B.O.S.S. and when she asks what this stands for they say 'Bad Omen Shift Shirker'.

Maia herself is becoming more withdrawn and less confident. Ben decides to see Maia to sort the situation out. The tack he takes with her is to 'buck her up' by saying that she needs to pull herself together, to answer back to team members when they tease her, to make sure she knows the rules and sticks to them. If there are any more mistakes or failures of procedure when she's on shift, he'll have to start disciplinary action. Maia bursts into tears, leaves the supervision meeting, takes a week off sick, then sends in a doctor's letter saying that she is under a lot of stress and needs a longer period of sick leave.

## What's going on?

| | | |
|---|---|---|
| Nature of difference | ▶ | An initial query about different styles of working, quickly built to scapegoating the different member of the team for all problems |
| Reasons for difference | ▶ | Styles of working<br>Attitudes to the client group<br>Value attached to working closely with clients |
| Any other factors | ▶ | Untrained manager<br>Particular team culture making it hard to break into<br>No proper induction |

## General comments

Scapegoating is an extremely common phenomenon in groups. It usually is an indicator of a malfunctioning group and if the issue is not brought into the open and addressed, will continue. Often the scapegoat has become essential to the continued operation of the group, and if one scapegoat leaves they will pick another one. Some common factors include:

- Some people seem to expect to become the focus for abuse and dislike in groups.
- Some scapegoats are chosen on the basis of visible differences.
- Scapegoating may be a technique which allows the group to stay together.
- Scapegoating may be used as a process to deal with those members who are seen to be delaying the progress of their peers.

As the group are laying the blame on to one team member's shoulders for some or all of the 'bad' or negative things that happen in the team, one of the first things to do is to expose this. There is also the attendant issue about who is allocated the role of scapegoat, this person's self-esteem, and what factors the team uses to pick the scapegoat. Quite often the person being scapegoated may not be in the best position to act to change matters, since they have already been allocated to a low and less powerful position in the team.

## Issues for managers

When the team manager becomes aware of scapegoating, good practice is to:

- Make the scapegoating visible to the whole team and the consequences of it.
- Strengthen the scapegoat.
- Monitor and change the pattern of dealing with negative issues that the team has evolved.

This is quite skilful team intervention and team building work, and if the team's own manager is not confident or is colluding in the team's scapegoating activities, then the issues should be picked up by a more senior staff member. This situation can be commonest when a manager has been appointed from within the team itself and has not been given adequate training. The process of becoming a manager from being an equal member of the team is not easy. It may also be compounded by general lack of management training or coaching from the organisation. Some warning bells for senior managers to watch out for:

- high turnover in a team (either 20% or more, or radically greater than other teams);
- rumours about a manager or about a team;
- high absence figures;
- more than the average number of 'critical incidents' reported;
- the team manager not addressing any issues directly in their own supervision;
- complaints or grievances from the team members or the clients;
- a radical change in morale.

In order to use these indicators, the organisation must be geared up to collect statistics and must have a good supervision system in operation. They are both in-built safety nets to allow senior staff to pick up areas that need attention and to deal with them.

## What the participants could do next

### Scapegoat

By the very nature of being made a scapegoat – someone who has less visible or perceived power in the group – the person affected will find it difficult to act. One common route out of disfunctioning teams is to make allegiances to protect oneself. However, that may not be a viable option in this case.

The staff member could:

- document all issues where they feel they are being unjustly blamed or treated;

- get the support of someone in a better position of power – the old team leader, the union rep, etc;
- make a formal complaint with particular documented incidents.

Senior staff find it much easier to respond to documented cases than general complaints of 'it's unfair' or 'I'm the one that always gets the blame'.

## Useful phrases

If you feel you are being scapegoated, try and spotlight what you think is happening, and ask for clarification.

'Why am I being singled out?'
'What exactly do you think I am not doing or saying?'
'I was not the one who left the door open ...' (or some such clear statement of fact when accused of doing something)
'What evidence do you have?'
'What are you basing that statement on?'

## Towards a more positive outcome

Scapegoating is an insidious and potentially damaging form of bullying that can turn highly competent staff into nervous wrecks lacking in self confidence and self-esteem.

- As a manager or as a colleague:

  Don't ignore scapegoating.
  Don't stand by as a team colleague and let it carry on.

- Exposing scapegoating is the first step to dealing with it.
- Focussing on how teams work, as well as what they work on, is just as important in helping them work better.

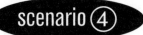

# INDIVIDUAL DIFFERENCES

## 4.1 Disagreement on facts and methods

At SafetyNet two of the welfare benefits advice workers, Tina and Migwe, have completely different attitudes to all aspect of the work, for example:

- the nature of advice work
- their expected level of involvement with clients
- how much detail to record on internal forms
- dealing with each other's clients
- taking time off in lieu (TOIL)
- expectations about flexibility and 'holding the fort'
- dedication to the job, etc.

They are not able to work well together – the situation is so bad that one of them won't say 'hello' to the other in the morning and won't ever volunteer to make the other a cup of coffee. If there is a disagreement about something in the advice centre it is predictable that they will be on opposing sides. This has been exacerbated by the debate on the future of the Centre. (See *Scenario 3.1.*) Now the Committee has bid for the regional advice delivery and got the contract. This change in way the advice centre works means that they do not have any choice in how they work any more. Tina's much more *laissez faire* and involved approach will have to change. Migwe feels completely vindicated – Tina feels very threatened.

They had developed a kind of *modus operandi,* avoiding each other as far as possible. However now there is no possibility of that – they have to work side by side and liaise closely over cases. Each time they disagree, the clash adds fuel to the bitterness of the conflict. (See 'episodes' model of conflict in *Chapter 2.*)

Brian, the Director, has tried to get them to work better together in the past – but his efforts only seem to make it worse. They actively dislike each other and do not bother to hide the fact. Brian has not had the time to document exactly how he wants the new system to run, but the average time spent with a client will have to come down and the way the contacts are reported has to change to fit in with the new local authority guidelines. Tina disagrees so strongly with this that she refuses to spend less time with people who she says genuinely need it. She encourages clients to come back as often as they like and spends time chatting with them as well as dealing with their difficulties. She also delves into other areas of their lives such as helping them get to and from hospital and the chiropodist.

Migwe has all sympathy for the clients, but sees that there are some people with needs who won't get seen at all if Tina continues as before, and that the Centre won't be funded for her work. The situation carries on for about a month with Tina refusing to adapt to the new scheme. Then Brian finds a detailed analysis of Tina's working hours and what she has spent her time on over the last month on his desk. Migwe has sent a copy to the Chair of the Committee and Tina as well.

He explains his actions as being on behalf of the clients and the service, as Tina seemed out to wreck the new scheme. Tina goes ballistic when she finds out and says that she can't work in such an environment. She goes home and the next week Brian gets a doctor's note signing her off for three weeks with 'stress'.

Brian gets in one of the locum advisers. While Tina is away even Brian, who is not noted for his sensitivity to atmosphere, realises that the tension levels in the office have dropped dramatically. The locum is so efficient that Brian wishes Tina would not come back to work so that he could employ this woman full time. He is tempted to try and use his position as manager to ensure this.

## What's going on?

Nature of difference ▶ Every aspect of being an advice worker
Inability to compromise with a colleague

Reasons for difference ▶ Values about advice work
Attitudes towards being flexible

Other factors ▶ Boundaries being drawn too flexibly by the manager
Agreed team standards are not followed
Too much personal preference is allowed
Manager letting a dispute get out of hand
Colleagues not being able to respect each other

## General comments

This type of action by Migwe is a sign of desperation. He would not have taken such drastic action without being very frustrated either with how the situation was being handled or the length of time it had taken to develop this far. Conflicts of this nature tend to build up over months, sometimes years, until there is a 'final straw'. This pushes one participant over the edge of being able to cope.

Tina cares about the work but is very inflexible when other people say that it either cannot or should not be carried out the way she wants to do it. Now she has gone off sick with 'stress'. Some conflicts carry such internal meaning for the people involved that they can't at some level operate without them. Tina is resistant to the new way of working and has effectively refused to co-operate.

Brian has not taken a very constructive line throughout the development of this situation. His approach to management is always to look for consensus, and recent distractions have meant he has not spent as much time managing the staff as he needs to. This is a good example of how managers need to act as soon as they are aware of difficulties and tensions building up in a team and get to the bottom of them. Some people need strong management otherwise they interpret a consensus approach as being an opportunity to get their own way. Lack of explicit boundaries means that they choose their own.

## Issues for managers

Managers in this sort of situation have to deal with the immediate fallout of the 'incident' – the way in which Migwe shopped Tina; Tina's performance; and the underlying need for clearer boundaries for all staff.

- Make quality standards clear from the start.
- Work on team difficulties before they get out of hand.
- Use the supervision mechanisms to lay down very strict guidelines for those staff who insist on interpreting the rules in a way different from yours.
- Use the disciplinary procedure if they still won't toe the line.
- Ensure that all discussions about the future direction of the organisation involve staff in consultation but not necessarily in thinking they can carry on trying to exert influence once the consultation has ended.

## What the participants could do

### The manager
Brian needs to make plain to Migwe that he acted out of order and that if he were going to make a complaint he should have come to Brian first. He asks Migwe if he wants to make a detailed complaint about Tina's work and attitudes to clients and show how it is affecting him by giving some incidents that have happened. Brian asks him to write these down and think about how he would like to see Tina change and how he could change to enable the team to work better together.

Brian also meets with the other advisers and goes over the team's guidelines on working practices, to re-establish professional boundaries. He writes to Tina telling her what he has done and inviting her to a meeting with him to discuss the situation when she gets back.

### The colleague (Migwe)
Migwe may have been at the end of his tether, but his action to unilaterally monitor another worker's hours and then give the information to the Chair of the Committee was not the best first course of action. He should have used the

internal complaints procedure first and worked with Brian and the rest of the team on how to deal with frustrations that were affecting the whole team, but crystallising into conflict between him and Tina.

### The colleague (Tina)

This type of worker needs to look at what she is expecting from a working environment; and to realise that she can't meet all clients' needs so that the workplace is a source of constant compromise. Brian needs to work with her on thinking through how she can work more constructively with colleagues and what she brings to the conflict, if her conflict pattern is always seeking to blame the other and take the moral high ground.

## Useful phrases

Brian will have to use his powers of persuasion, influence and authority to tackle this problem. For example with Tina:

'This is an example of the level of detail I need for the client record sheets. Is this clear? I'd like to look through your records at the end of the week – just to check you've got the hang of it.'

'If you are having trouble prioritising work, then let's talk about it.'

'I know that you and Migwe have different ideas, but this is how we have to work now, and it is not negotiable.'

Or with Migwe:

'Leaving the memo about Tina's hours on my desk was one thing – passing it to the Committee implies that you have no trust in my ability to act on this. Is this the case?'

'If you have a difficulty with another staff member I'd like you to try and sort it out between you first. If that is not possible, then come to me.'

## Towards a more positive outcome

This case turned into a complex conflict with serious outcomes and stand-offs because it had been allowed to escalate out of all proportion.

- Brian needs to agree a plan with the Chair of the Committee to bring the current advice work into line with the new working practices.
- He can then deal with any individual who does not work to the guidelines through supervision and, if necessary, the disciplinary procedure.
- Disputes like this between staff may seem petty and childish, but if they are not dealt with, they can grow into huge resentments. The layers of grievance then build up until they become very hard to untangle.
- However frustrated the manager is, they must not be tempted to use sickness as an excuse to 'get rid of' staff.

# 4.2 Differences in values and disrespect

At Ranch Hostel, team leader Ben is getting into a difficult relationship with the finance worker over how to fill in expense claims. The finance worker, Max, has strict rules about how expense claims forms are to be filled in and what amounts need receipts etc. Max has instituted these new rules in the last three months and each time that Ben has sent in his forms they have been wrong or inadequate in some way. Max is lower down the hierarchy at Ranch Hostel than Ben and is feeling slighted by what he perceives to be Ben's cavalier attitude. He is beginning to wonder if this failure on Ben's part is deliberate.

Max sets up a meeting with Ben and his team to go through the forms and the correct procedures. He sets it up at some inconvenience to himself and agrees to go out to the hostel office to do the work. Owing to a breakdown in communication he arrives just as the team meeting is finishing. The team members all have to be somewhere else and disappear. Max has wasted his whole morning. He bites his tongue and does not blame Ben outright for this mess up. He goes back to the main office and writes a very clear and detailed memo about the correct procedures. For the next three months the forms are correctly completed. Max does not immediately realise that this is because Ben has delegated the work to his deputy. Max relaxes his vigilance and hopes that the issue is now sorted.

It is now approaching the end of the financial year returns and Max sends out for more detailed financial information. Ben is the last team leader to send in his information – which is of course inaccurate and wrong. Ben not getting his figures in on time means Max has to work at the weekend. Max mentions this to the Director at their next supervision and the Director is surprisingly unwilling to believe that Ben is as bad as Max makes out. He laughs it off as, 'That's Ben all over – brilliant with the clients and bad at the detail!' Max is very surprised by this and makes no comment at the time except to say again that he resented having to work over the weekend and it's him that will be in trouble with the auditors, not Ben.

Ben's expenses claims are back to being inaccurately filled in three months later and Max tries again to set up a meeting to go through the procedure. He arrives at the hostel just as Ben is leaving to handle an emergency in a second hostel. Max ends up in a complete state and accuses Ben of deliberately manipulating him and making his life a misery.

Max again raises with the Director how difficult he is finding working with Ben. The next week Max finds that he is summoned to a meeting to answer claims that he was swearing at Ben and undermining his authority in front of his staff. Now Max feels completely stuck in a nightmare not of his own making.

## What's going on?

Nature of the difference ▶ Value of hostel work versus finance work
Importance of following procedures
Attitudes to detailed work

Reasons for difference ▶ Approach to work
Skills

Any other factors ▶ Director being biassed
Lack of respect for specialist skills
Difficulties in the line management structure
Lack of understanding of finance work

## General comments

There are two main issues here. The first is that in Ranch Hostel, hostel and housing work is seen as the most important type of work. Resourcing the hostel work is a very secondary function and the Director does not help hostel staff understand how important it is. The second issue is that of not setting clear boundaries of management responsibility. Max is junior to Ben and does not manage staff. They both report to the Director. It has not been made clear how much authority Max has in finance matters to instruct managers who are technically more senior than him. Boundaries of line responsibility are important to keep clear between all levels of staff. If they are not made explicit then staff tend to interpret them as they want to in their own favour. This can lead to different interpretations of:

- content of job descriptions;
- responsibility for tasks;
- nature and purpose of meetings;
- who can complain about whose work to whom;
- what happens when workers do not carry out legitimate instructions from a member of staff with specialist knowledge if they are not in a direct line relationship to them.

In this case the finance worker's task is being made difficult by the failure of a hostel team leader to act in line with reporting requirements. The team leader is technically senior in standing to the finance worker, but for the purposes of this piece of work the finance worker needs to call the tune. The hostel team leader then effectively obstructs the finance worker's attempts to sort out the issues and uses his power as a hostel team leader to influence his view of what is going on in this case.

It is very common that organisations in the voluntary sector have a service delivery side and a resourcing side. Both sides need each other to work well to make the whole organisation run properly. In well managed organisations, senior staff are able and willing to point out how both parts need the other and do not let this particular value issue get out of hand. However, where the Director is a service delivery specialist in an organisation that does not deal with rivalries or value-laden status issues such as this one, bitter conflicts and inefficiencies can arise.

## Issues for managers

- Be very clear about line management boundaries.
- Be clear about boundaries concerning a line manager working with a person across a hierarchical boundary.
- Do not let line managers off the hook about procedures that matter to organisational effectiveness.
- Senior staff should be involved in setting quality standards and deadlines for reporting so that junior members of staff are not put in the invidious position of hassling a member of staff who is senior to them.

## What the participants could do

### Max

He has tried an informal approach and not succeeded – so he has two choices now. He can go for a formal approach and make a written complaint both about Ben's lack of respect for his guidelines and the manager's handling of the events. This would have to go to the Committee. This strategy carries some risks. The Committee may be reluctant to get involved; they may not have the skills to deal with a complaint of this nature; there may not be a procedure in place for them to use; they may shy away from being involved in a process that could upset the always delicate balance between Committee and the Director. Max may not end up getting what he wants out of the complaint. However at least he will have registered his protest and got his side of events documented.

He can gather evidence of the failure of Ben to deliver to deadlines, begin to put all requests in writing and dated. He can try and gain allies in giving more authority to his case, for example, the Treasurer.

If he ends up getting a verbal warning as a result of being summoned to the disciplinary meeting, he can appeal against that and have his side of the story heard by the Director in this formal way.

If none of these work, he can go to his union representative for support. Indeed he could have them present at the disciplinary meeting.

## Useful phrases

When entering into a difficult meeting which you foresee has the potential to become a conflict situation it is wise to be prepared – to know what you will compromise on and what you won't. If situations or comments are 'sprung' on you, take time to think if necessary. You could also comment on the unfortunate timing and suggest a discussion at a later stage when you have had time to think.

Prepare:

- Think through your position.
- Think through statements and make sure they are couched in language that is not inflammatory or potentially offensive.

First phase:

- Ask for clarification.
- Paraphrase the other's position to make sure you have understood it.
- Don't make assumptions about the other's position or reasons for it – ask!
- Create space.
- Say that you need time to think if you do and set realistic deadlines for a second meeting.

Remember that if you have gained one or two more insights into the other person's views or position, then you are making progress. It may take several meetings to get to a final position that is appropriate and comfortable for both sides.

## Towards a more positive outcome

For the staff member just trying to do their job as effectively as they can, a situation of being stymied by one person and then dismissed by the person who should be in a position to sort out the difficulty is very difficult.

- Put issues in writing to clarify them and show how seriously you take them.
- Try and gain support from other staff who are in a position to see what is going on.
- Managers are not always as skilled as we would like them to be and strongly dislike having their faults pointed out to their face.
- If you are being managed by an inexperienced manager it may be a case for showing them a course of action that they can feel good about, diplomatically.

For the Director faced with what might seem at first glance to be an irritating and very procedural issue:

- If the problem of poor performance affects a person in the organisation who you are seen not to value, you must act very carefully to offset any accusations of favouritism and indeed acting in a biassed way.
- It might be wise to involve a neutral person to look at the complaint rather than dismissing it out of hand. Involve a member of the Management Committee as a safeguard.

# 4.3 Personality clash

Avril and Sunil are both advisers at SafetyNet, the locally-based advice centre. They have both been in post about 12 months, and on a day-to-day basis have had little to do with each other directly except in team meetings. Avril specialises in money advice and Sunil in Welfare Benefits. They don't particularly get on, and are at different stages in what they want from work in general and from this job in particular. They also have very different personalities. Avril is patient and likes time to think things over, whereas Sunil often has quick solutions. He has a 'right answer' most of the time and can easily appear bored with staff meetings if they don't 'go his way'.

Now they have been asked by Sam, the deputy manager, to review the confidentiality policy for SafetyNet. After the first meeting it rapidly becomes clear to Avril that she is not going to enjoy this piece of work. Sunil breezed into the meeting, assumed that he would do the bulk of the work, that confidentiality was straightforward, any fool could work it out by common sense and if they couldn't they shouldn't be working here, etc. Avril tried to get a word in edgeways, but gave up pretty soon. She suggested that he draft the policy and then she would comment on the draft in writing before the next meeting as that would be the most efficient way to take it forward.

The evening before their next meeting she finds what she considers to be a scrappy draft of the confidentiality policy in her tray. She has no time to go through it in her careful way. The next thing to irritate her is that Sunil turns up ten minutes late for the meeting and opens by saying he has to go somewhere else in half an hour and what did she think of it. Avril was irritated by his lateness anyway and now by this approach which she perceives as inefficient – he should have given plenty of time for the meeting. She interprets this as lacking in respect of her needs and ways of working. Sunil rapidly gets impatient with her in speech and body language when she says that he hasn't done what he said he would and she hasn't had time to consider her response. He makes a comment about 'no time for perfectionism and they need to get it finished by the end of the week'. She replies that this untidy effort wouldn't get them many good conduct points and she for one is not prepared to turn in incomplete or inaccurate work. Sunil takes offence at this and grabs it back off her and storms out. They both end up going to the Director, Brian, separately and complaining about the other's behaviour.

Brian is deeply pre-occupied at the present with the local government funding changes and just needs them to get the work done. He agrees with Sunil that Avril can be a perfectionist and with Avril that Sunil can be irritating. They both interpret this as Brian being 'on their side'. The next time they meet they continue to irritate each other and end up coming out with, 'Brian agrees with me that you're a perfectionist', 'Well, he said to me that you're irritating'. This is of course not helpful to team relationships. It inflames their suspicions about unfair treatment and lack of confidentiality on Brian's part. They both suspect Brian is guilty of discussing their attributes behind each other's backs. Now they go off and each tell their best friend in the team what has been happening from their perspective. They manage to further entrench their dislike of each other and more importantly their inability to work together.

## What's going on?

Nature of difference ▸ Methods of working
Use of deadlines and time for comments

Reasons for difference ▸ Different styles of working
Perceived lack of respect on Sunil's part
Lack of clarity about deadlines on Avril's part

Any other factors ▸ No particular loyalty to each other to get the task done in a way that respects and accommodates each other's way of working
Personality clash

## General comments

It is incredibly easy for workers to annoy and irritate each other for no other reasons than personal style and personality differences. Unfortunately these types of differences are inherent and neither is right or wrong. What may be a management issue is how these differences come to affect the relationship between the individuals and how this might spill over into the rest of the team.

Each party may be brought to an understanding of the other's perspective, but they won't be able to change their natural response to tasks. However, they can be taught skills that mean they are more likely to be able to work effectively together.

## Issues for managers

In cases like this it is crucial for mangers to intervene sooner rather than later.

- Make clearer the process issues in the team. Point out that different skills and abilities are important in getting a good outcome.
- Foster team loyalty.
- Foster each team member's understanding of the preferred way of working of the others.
- Do not let team members ignore normal team rules or boundaries, just to accommodate personal preferences.
- Make the best of each person's skills and allocate tasks appropriately.
- Give opportunities to develop skills that move away from inherent preferences, but with support for achievement, not punishment for failure.

## What participants could do next

Brian was understandably distracted when the team members came to see him. However, by not paying proper attention to them, he has made the situation worse. Any manager makes mistakes sometimes and especially when they are distracted by issues that affect the whole future of the organisation. However, a manager's lot is never a happy one and Brian cannot afford to neglect this seemingly trivial dispute between two of his advice staff. One reason is that if he does he runs the risk of the whole incident blowing up out of proportion, a perfect example of the 'fire' model of conflict (see *Chapter 2*). Another risk is that with all the turmoil going on anyway in the team (see *Scenario 3.1*), he doesn't need another excuse for a clique developing. One approach would be:

1   See Avril and Sunil separately to let them blow off steam. Get down on paper exactly what the issues are.

2   Ask them to go away and think about what they want to see happen in the situation to improve their working relationship. Ask them, for example, what they are prepared to change about their way of working and what changes would they like to see in the other person's way of working. This ensures that they see that change is needed on both sides rather than giving in to the temptation to think that the other is always the one totally at fault.

3   Once the replies are in, discuss them separately again and then together to work out a compromise position.

4   Stress that you expect them to stick to any agreement and not to come running to you every five minutes if the other one does something unacceptable. You will supervise them every three weeks instead of every six for the next two months and expect them to work hard on making the arrangement succeed.

## Useful phrases

'What are your strengths and what are X's strengths?'

'How can you work together with X better?'

'I realise you find X a perfectionist – but there are good points about that skill. It is not appropriate for you to keep up a series of jokes about her in the coffee room.'

'This team needs all sorts of people in it and you and your skills are no better than X and her skills.'

## Towards a more positive outcome

The manager could use Belbin's team roles exercise (see *Chapter 3*) to demonstrate how they have different strengths – with the rest of the team members. This might also give them an appreciation of each other's worth to the team as a whole and how an effective team needs workers with different styles and strengths.

- Do not neglect staff relationships. If a relationship is going wrong and affecting the way the participants or other staff are working, then a manager has a legitimate reason to insist that it changes. It is appropriate to notice and talk about these things where work or team work is being affected.
- Always listen to staff when they come to you with what seem trivial issues. They are important to the people concerned. At the same time it is important to try and not act as a referee – but to give those concerned the skills to sort out their own relationship problems. Otherwise they might come running to you with every little real or imagined slur.
- Use the supervision process to discuss team relationships – their problems and how they can be improved from the perspective of different members of staff.
- Even when other matters are very pressing never make comments to one staff member about another's habits or skills.

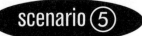

# CHANGE MANAGEMENT

## 5.1 A 'stuck' organisation with a new chair

Care4U's view of itself as a well-run organisation with excellent community standing and reputation has been frequently threatened over the last six months. (*See Scenarios 1.2, 1.3, 2.1.*) Martha, the Chief Executive, has had to spend more time on internal management matters than she would normally do. She prefers to spend her time at a political level, getting and securing opportunities for Care4U in the local area. She is excellent at networking and making those all important funding contacts. However, even she has to recognise that all is not well with her senior and middle managers. There have been incidents over the last six months that have thrown up:

- inappropriate boundaries between managers and their staff;
- poor induction programmes for new managers;
- no emphasis on getting a strong team at senior or middle management level;
- no emphasis on developing organisational management performance standards that are regularly assessed;
- accusations of racism;
- accusation of taking on funds for a service that Care4U was not equipped to deliver and delivered badly;
- breaches in health and safety mechanisms;
- poor industrial relations;
- an Employment Tribunal case settled out of court.

Now the middle managers have written as a group to Martha, detailing what they see as poor management practice and inappropriate value systems in the organisation. They are suggesting a complete review of management operations. Martha's initial reaction is to reject all these points as a deliberate slur on her good name and to carry on as usual. She has a meeting with the managers saying that basically they are trying to undermine her and if any word of this gets out they'll be dismissed for breaking Care4U rules on confidentiality. She refuses to listen to their well-reasoned points.

The managers' report is then leaked to the senior managers and the Chair of the Executive Committee, an old friend of Martha's. The Chair of the Committee comes into the organisation to stress that these have been a difficult few months, but that this is a complete over-reaction and Care4U is very well respected in the community.

The managers feel very stuck after this meeting and do not know what to do next. The two remaining senior managers are split. One is for taking this seriously and one is for carrying on as normal – the third post is vacant pending the recruitment of a new Assistant Director, Finance. Nothing much happens for three months until the new ADF is recruited and the Chair resigns owing to poor health. The new Chair was the old Vice-Chair and had seen the difficulties arising in Care4U. He is an ex-Housing Association senior manager, who knows about the importance of management structures.

The new Chair decides to take on the Chief Executive and insist on changes to management practices under the guise of reviewing quality outputs across the organisation. Kwame, the new Assistant Director, Finance is horrified to find out what has been going on in the past and is a great voice for change at the senior management level.

Martha feels under siege from her Chair and her managers and agrees reluctantly to a review of management practices, initially to be carried out by the Chair of the Committee.

## What's going on?

Nature of difference   ▶   Management practices
Balance of internal vs external focus of Chief Executive

Reasons for difference   ▶   Different stress levels in the hierarchy
Different perceptions of the effects of poor
   management

Any other factors   ▶   Recent disciplinary cases
Organisational value system questioned
Lack of focus on diversity issues

## General comments

The competence of the Chief Executive is important in all organisations, not least in the voluntary sector. A great deal is expected of them as competent internal managers and external networkers. They are expected to have good leadership qualities and to balance the needs of the Committee and the staff. The Chief Executive's role is often a lonely one and it is very difficult to be successful in all areas. If a person is recruited who has strong qualities in raising the external profile and that is where the bulk of their interests and talents lie, then it is very tempting to recruit them.

However all organisations need a balance of competence in both delivering the service and internal management practices. If the Chief Executive is ignoring or glossing over difficulties of such a scale in management practices, it jeopardises the future of the whole organisation. It is possible for organisations to carry on without attending to management issues, but they are often very vulnerable to either incompetent or possibly corrupt practices at all levels. Good management safeguards organisations against such problems.

Change management is not easy when the key decision makers are blocking action – even in the face of overwhelming evidence. In this case it was only when two key decision makers changed in the organisation that progress could be made in the teeth of such strong opposition.

## Issues for managers

Even if the need for change is blindingly obvious to some people in the organisation, there are going to be powerful vested interests against change. Change is never comfortable and for some managers it will be threatening. They may have to learn new skills or alter habits, and this may imply that they are not good at their job. When they have not been supervised in a constructive way or perhaps in any way this will lead some managers to be very resentful and possibly to actively wreck any change process. It will be important to:

- use all influence possible to promote a debate about what is wrong;
- gather hard facts about key indicators, for example staff turnover or staff absence;
- make the arguments over and over again;
- persevere against opposition;
- get allies on the Committee and at all levels.

Using other pegs to hang change on can make it more respectable and attractive – for example:

- Quality Assurance schemes
- Investors in People programmes.

Resistance can be heartfelt until a critical mass is reached by staff turnover or persuasion. If this seems to be taking too long for the health of the organisation, then getting an outsider to give an honest and skilled assessment can be useful.

## What the participants could do next

### New Chair

The Chair of any organisation is a key influencing factor on what decisions are made. They are the linchpin and if they are not in favour of the change or are influenced away from it by other powerful key people – nothing significant will happen. Now the new Chair is in favour of reviewing management practices and can see what is wrong with the current structure, progress can be made. They will need to work carefully with the Chief Executive to help her to see her role in a different light and to work on a new balance of internal and external involvement in Care4U.

### Senior managers

The senior management group are also key players as they will have to make significant changes to the way they work. They will become subject to supervision and will be required to institute changes down the structure in the teams they manage. They need to be worked with to ensure that they are fully behind the change and can see benefits for themselves as well as for the organisation.

### Middle managers

Middle or line managers are the next key group of people – they manage at the front end of the service delivery and will need to see the benefits for them of change. These will be different from the ones for senior staff.

## Useful phrases

The communication skills most useful in this sort of conflict and change management are persuasion and persistence. This may require different approaches with different groups or stakeholders in Care4U. For example:

'If we go for a quality-assurance scheme like Investors in People it will increase our credibility with funders.'

'Please come on the Investors in People working group – then you can get your comments heard where they can do most good.'

'Don't carp about the failings of the senior staff – what about the influence of the Committee in all this?'

'If we have a high staff turnover because managers aren't doing their job properly – it's like burning money – each recruitment costs us £2000.'

## Towards a more positive outcome.

When whole organisations are in conflict over change it can be an exceptionally difficult environment; however it can be creative and exciting as well. People don't like change and find it stressful – don't spring surprises on them and you'll have more chance of success.

Once a critical mass of key decision makers are in favour of change:

- Decide a process and strategy for change.
- Ensure that the Committee fully support the change process and are prepared to resource it as necessary.
- Ensure consultation is carried out effectively – but not to the nth degree.
- Be willing to see changes through – and recognise that it will take time.
- Establish some key indicators of success early on in the process and monitor them regularly so that you know progress is being made.

# APPENDIX

## Noticing patterns

Try filling in this chart – going through some of your personal patterns in relation to conflict.

| MY CULTURE/HISTORY | MY ATTITUDES/BELIEFS | MY POWER |
|---|---|---|
| MY LABEL | COMMUNICATION STYLE | HEAD MESSAGES<br><br>PERCEIVED PERSONAL COST |
| ORGANISATION STUFF | | ENVIRONMENT |
| MY PREFERRED RESPONSE: | | |

**SAMPLE CHART**

| MY CULTURE/HISTORY | MY ATTITUDES/BELIEFS | MY POWER |
|---|---|---|
| I hate anger. | Men are more aggressive than women in communication. | I'm white.<br>  able-bodied.<br>  a woman. |
| I don't know how to respond if I feel someone is criticising me. | I am not assertive. | I'm not a manager. |
| I can see myself blush in a difficult meeting. | Women get more rewards if they are assertive. | |

| MY LABEL | COMMUNICATION STYLE | HEAD MESSAGES |
|---|---|---|
| I give myself a 'helper' label. | I talk about 'getting hold of things'. | |
| I think others take me for granted and see me as someone without strong opinions because I don't take part in conflicts. | I lose my temper.<br><br>When I'm in a mood people know it. | PERCEIVED PERSONAL COST |

| ORGANISATION STUFF | | ENVIRONMENT |
|---|---|---|
| | | |

**MY PREFERRED RESPONSE:**

I label others as the 'problem'.

I work hard to avoid conflict situations.

I dislike staff meetings where I think conflict will erupt.

I am fearful of being personally verbally attacked.

I find it hard to put forward what I really think in case it is challenged.

I'm stuck.

I have an Inner judge – not an Inner advocate.

# FURTHER READING

## Managing conflict

*A Sudden Outbreak of Common Sense*, Andrew Acland, London Century Press, 1990

*Constructive Conflict Management*, John Crawley, Nb Publishing, 1992
(ISBN 1 85788 014 5, £14.99)

*From stalemate to synergy: the workplace mediation manual*, Zanne Findlay and Carl Reynolds, Hill Top publishing, 1997
(ISBN 0 9531099 09 available from Hill Top Publishing, 207 Waller Rd, London SE14 5LX, £22)

*Playing with Fire*, Nic Fine and Fiona Macbeth, Youth Work Press, National Youth Agency, 17–23 Albion St, Leicester, LE1 6DG
(ISBN 0 86155 141 9, £14.95)

'Handling Conflict' in *From Strength to Strength*, Maggie Jardine, National Youth Agency, 1987, (NYA, 17–23 Albion St, Leicester, LE1 6DG
(ISBN 0 86155 110 9, £4.95)

'Managing differences and conflict' in *Just about Managing*, 3rd Edition, Sandy Adirondack, LVSC, 1998 (ISBN 1 872582 17 6, £14.95)

## Teams as groups

*Understanding Organisations*, Charles Handy, Penguin Business Books, 1985 (ISBN 0 14 009110 6)

*Understanding Voluntary Organisations*, Charles Handy, Penguin Business Books, 1988 (ISBN 0 14 022491 2)

*Management teams: why they succeed or fail*, R Meredith Belbin, Heinneman Professional Publishing, 1981

*The Successful Self*, Dorothy Rowe, HarperCollins, 1988
(ISBN 0 00 637342 9)

*Victims of Group Think, A psychological study of foreign policy*, L Janis, 1977

## Communication and dealing with discrimination

*Everyday Acts against racism – raising children in a multi-racial world*, Ed Maureen T Reddy, Seal Press, 1997 (ISBN 1 878067 85 0, £12.99)

*Understanding diversity; readings, cases and exercises*, Carol Harvey and M June Allard, HarperCollins (ISBN 0 673 46996 4)

*How to talk so kids will listen and listen so kids will talk*, Adele Faber and Elaine Mazlish (ISBN 0 380 57000 9)

*Siblings without rivalry*, Adele Faber and Elaine Mazlish

## Bullying

*Bullying at work – How to confront and overcome it*, Andrea Adams, Virago Press, £7.99

*How big is the problem of Bullying at work?* Survey report from MSF research, MSF Centre, 33–37 Moreland St, London EC1V 8PB

## Violence at work

*Health and Safety Handbook*, Directory of Social Change, 1998 (ISBN 1 900360 25 X, £12.50)

*Handling Aggression and Violence at work, a Training Manual*, David Leadbetter and Robin Trewitha, Russell House Press, Russell House, Lyme Close, Lyme Regis, Dorset, DT7 3DE (ISBN 1 898924 65 1)

*Office Health and Safety*, City Centre, 32–35 Featherstone St, London, EC1Y 8QX

# RESOURCES

Please note that from 22 April 2000, telephone numbers will officially change in London. Where applicable, new numbers are given in brackets. In the changeover period from June 1999 to August/September 2000, either number can be used.

Health and Safety Executive
HSE Information Centre
Broad Lane
Sheffield
S3 7HQ
0541 545500

Victim Support
National Office
Cranmer House
39 Brixton Rd
London
SW9 6DZ
0171 735 9166 (0207 735 9166)

Public Concern at work
Suite 306
16 Baldwin's Gdns
London
EC1N 7RJ
0171 404 6609 (0207 404 6609)
*Supports employees who are concerned about malpractice at work.*

Mediation UK
Alexander House
Telephone Avenue
Bristol
BS1 4BS
0117 904 6661
*Information and advice on all kinds of Mediation. Publishes a directory of trainers in mediation £6.00.*

Mediation Service
National Centre for Voluntary Organisations (NCVO)
Regent's Wharf
8 All Saints St
London
N1 9RL
0171 713 6161 (0207 713 6161)
Helpdesk for information on mediation service: 0845 600 4500
*Able to supply skilled mediators, experienced in the voluntary sector.*
*NCVO also publishes a directory of management consultants.*

Leap Confronting Conflict
8 Lennox Rd
London
N4 3NW
0171 272 5630 (0207 272 5630)
*Runs conflict resolution courses and able to supply trainers in-house for all aspects of conflict resolution. Supplies* Playing with Fire *and other texts on youth and conflict resolution.*

Management Development Network
39 Gabriel House
Odessa St
London
SE16 1HQ
0171 232 0726 (0207 232 0726)
*Supplies a directory of management consultants specialising in the voluntary sector.*

National Youth Agency
17–23 Albion St
Leicester
LE1 6GD
0116 285 6789
*Publishes and supplies interesting handbooks, resources and magazines for youth workers. Has a library and information centre.*

Conflict Management Plus
The Cottage
102 High St
Barkway
Royston
Herts
SG8 8ES
01763 849600
*Supplies* Constructive Conflict Management *and runs training on constructive conflict management skills.*

Advisory, Conciliation & Arbitration Service (ACAS)
27 Wilton St
London
SW1X 7AZ
0171 210 3659 (0207 210 3659)
*Gives advice on conflicts and disciplinary procedures or industrial disputes. Can provide impartial third parties such as conciliators or mediators.*